Active Learning for Children with Disabilities

A Manual for Use with the Active Learning Series

Pam Bailey

with

Debby Cryer

Thelma Harms

Sheri Osborne

Barbara A. Kniest

Innovative Learning Publications

Addison-Wesley Publishing Company

Menlo Park, California • Reading, Massachusetts • New York
Don Mills, Ontario • Wokingham, England • Amsterdam • Bonn
Paris • Milan • Madrid • Sydney • Singapore • Tokyo
Seoul • Taipei • Mexico City • San Juan

This book is published by Innovative Learning Publications™, an imprint of the Alternative Publishing Group of Addison-Wesley Publishing Company.

Senior Editor: Lois Fowkes
Design Manager: Jeff Kelly
Production/Manufacturing: Leanne Collins
Cover design: Paula Shuhert
Text design: Francesca Angelesco
Cover illustration: Jane McCreary

This publication was developed by the authors under contract with Child Development Resources, Inc. as part of the SpecialCare Project, grant number H024B00113 from the U.S. Department of Education, Early Education Program for Children with Disabilities. Points of view or opinions do not, however, necessarily represent official views or opinions of the Department of Education.

Duplo and Lego are registered trademarks of Interlego, A. G. Zug, Switzerland.

ISBN 0-201-49402-7
2 3 4 5 6 7 8 9 10-ML-98 97

Acknowledgments

The authors express their sincere appreciation to the following people:

Debra Hatton and Robin McWilliam for their insights into serving young children with disabilities; Corinne W. Garland for her editorial assistance with the manuscript;

field reviewers:
Lisa Rogers, Child Development Resources
Fran Scott, Child Development Resources
Debra Carlotti, VCU Day Care and Kindergarten
Phyllis Hoffman, Frank Porter Graham Child Development Center;

and field testers:
Laurene Harrold, CDR First Steps Child Care and Development Center
Linda Kelly, CDR First Steps Child Care and Development Center
Louise V. Denkins, Bright Horizons Learning Center
Shawna Walton, Bright Horizons Learning Center
B. L. Perry, Family provider/parent
Patricia C. Powell, Family provider/parent.

Contents

Using This Manual with the Active Learning Series

Your decision to include children with disabilities in your child-care setting is a good one. Everyone will benefit—children with disabilities, typically developing children, families, and caregivers.

The purpose of this manual is to provide information on and activities for infants, toddlers, and preschoolers with disabilities so that you can include them in all aspects of your childcare program. It is built upon the Active Learning Series curriculum. The Active Learning Series is made up of activity books for infants, one-, two-, and three-year-olds. (See *When You Want to Know More,* page 139.) Active Learning books for four- and five-year-olds are planned for publication in late 1995. This manual will apply to these books as well as the first four. Each one of these books contains a planning guide and four activity sections. The information and the activities in the series are useful for all children, both those with disabilities and those who are developing typically. Setting up your program as recommended in the Active Learning Series provides an excellent foundation for including children with disabilities, and this book gives additional support and specific ideas.

Children with disabilities are just like other children in most ways. You won't drastically need to change the way you do things just because a child with a disability is entering your program. Most of the time, you will only need to take the following steps:

- Plan each day's activities to include those children with disabilities, making changes as needed.
- Arrange the child-care setting and playground so that children with disabilities can be with other children and take part in all activities.
- Change some materials and activities so that children with disabilities can use them.

By reading this manual, you will learn about children with disabilities and how to include them in daily activities. Much of the information in this manual will be useful for typically developing children, too.

Where Do I Begin?

If you are already using the Active Learning Series, begin by reading this manual. The first major section contains information that is useful for planning for children with different kinds of disabilities. It contains tips on how to change the surroundings so that all the children can move about in the room and on the playground with confidence and how to adapt materials and activities for use with a wide range of abilities. It will also help you find activities that are right for the child with disabilities. The second major section is about specific types of disabilities. If you know the types of disabilities children you care for may have, you can read just those sections.

If you are not familiar with the Active Learning Series, begin by reviewing the activity books that are for the ages of the children in your care. You will notice that each activity book contains a section on planning for children in a specific age group, followed by sections addressing four different kinds of activities: listening and talking, physical development, creativity, and learning about the world. Notice that the section on planning includes information about relating to children, planning the day, and setting up the room. It also contains some information about the skills of typically developing children at each age and how to choose activities for them. The four activity sections contain information about why each type of activity is important, suggestions for materials, and a checklist to make sure that you make the most out of the activities while keeping them safe and fun. Once you are familiar with the Active Learning Series and perhaps have tried out some of the activities with the children in your care, you are ready to use this manual to help you adapt the Active Learning Series so that children with disabilities can join in the fun.

Quality Care for Children with Disabilities

KEY POINTS

- Everyone benefits when children with disabilities are included in child-care settings.

- Many specialists may be involved in the care of young children with disabilities.

- Parents and caregivers make the biggest contribution to the care of a child with disabilities.

Helping Young Children with Disabilities Learn Through Play

When you have watched children play, you probably have noticed the many ways they use their senses—touching, seeing, hearing, smelling, and tasting—to explore the world around them. In the sandbox, babies will feel sand with their hands and may try to put sand in their mouths. Some children will squiggle their feet deep under the sand, others will take a fistful of sand and let it sift through their fingers. Some children will build roads for toy trucks, others may enjoy burying toys under the sand just to dig them up again! Each child is learning something about the world while playing. The baby learns that the gritty sand is not for eating. The boy pushing his feet into the sand learns that it gets harder to move them as they go deeper into the sand. The girl watching sand sift through her fingers learns that sand is made of tiny grains, and when they fall, the grains roll over each other, making a little mound with a point on top. By sifting sand through her fingers time and time again, she learns the best way to hold her hand so that the sand forms the shape she wants. This learning helps children become ready for other learning that will come later.

Disabilities can keep children from playing and learning in the same way that typically developing children do. The child who cannot control his muscles will have trouble pushing his feet into the sand and holding them still while he builds a sand house. He may knock his sand house down before he ever gets the chance to realize that wet sand makes houses and dry sand doesn't. He may need help getting to the sandbox. A girl with impaired sight may enjoy feeling the sand sift through her fingers, but she may not be able to see the little mound that grows as the grains hit the ground. Both children need extra help if they are to learn the same things from playing as typically developing children do. *That is what this manual is all about—helping very young children with disabilities learn through play.*

Meeting Individual Needs — You Already Do It!

You might be a little nervous about caring for children with disabilities. Most people who are new at it are. But children with disabilities are just like other children in most ways—they need a safe and interesting place to play, time with a loving adult, and opportunities to play with other children.

Caregivers make sure that the individual needs of young children are met. You are meeting individual needs when you help a two-year-old in the bathroom, but let a three-year-old be more independent. You are meeting individual needs when you gently push one child on the swing while encouraging another to pump his legs. Meeting the needs of children with disabilities is much the same as meeting the needs of typically developing children because you treat each child individually, taking into account what the child can already do and what the child needs help learning to do.

Laws and Children with Disabilities

In the United States, including children with disabilities in child-care settings is so important that laws have been passed to make sure that children get the services they need. In 1972 the Economic Opportunity Act was changed to require that all Head Start programs reserve 10% of their enrollment slots for children with disabilities. Public Law 94-142, passed in 1975, guaranteed children with disabilities from age 5 to 21 the same educational rights as typically developing children—a free appropriate education. This law was amended in 1986 (Public Law 99-457) to require schools to serve 3- and 4-year-old children with disabilities. It also urged states to provide services to children with disabilities from birth. This law emphasized the importance of serving the families of children with disabilities. In 1991 this law was renamed the Individuals with Disabilities Education Act (IDEA).

The Americans with Disabilities Act (ADA) of 1990 requires that all public services be accessible to people with disabilities. This means that children with disabilities have the right to participate in the same play and learning activities as typically developing children. The law also means that public buildings, including child-care centers, must be accessible to persons with disabilities. This means that no child-care setting can turn away a child just because he or she has a disability and that reasonable modifications to the building, such as adding ramps, must be made to accommodate the needs of children with disabilities.

What Are Inclusive Child-Care Settings?

An important concept in both Public Law 94-142 and Public Law 99-457 is that a child can be cared for in the *least restrictive environment.* This term means that children with disabilities should as much as possible receive services along with typically developing children. Instead of providing services to children with disabilities in separate settings, children with disabilities should whenever possible attend the same schools, learn in the same classrooms, and attend the same child-care programs as typically developing children. Services provided to all children together are said to be *inclusive.* An inclusive child-care setting provides opportunities for all children—with and without disabilities—to play, learn, and get along with each other. An inclusive setting is the very best place for young children to learn. Why?

Everyone benefits from inclusive child-care. When children with and without disabilities learn together, the children, their parents, and the caregivers all benefit. Children with disabilities can make friends with other children and learn new skills from them. Because they take part in the same activities as typically developing children, they learn that they belong and are accepted. Children with disabilities who attend inclusive child-care programs develop independence and good feelings about themselves and what they can do. All children learn new ways to make friends as they play and talk with children with different abilities. They also learn to appreciate their own abilities in a new way and to accept and enjoy people who are not exactly like themselves.

When inclusive child-care settings were a new idea, some people were concerned that typically developing children would copy the behaviors of children with disabilities. In fact, these people had nothing to worry about because it actually worked the other way around. With some adult help, children with disabilities learned the behaviors of the other children in the child-care setting.

Over the years, a lot has been learned about what happens to children who are in inclusive child-care settings. In the chart below, you'll find a list of the myths about inclusive child-care settings and the true facts.

Myth	Fact
Typically developing children copy the behaviors of children with disabilities.	Some children might experiment with new behaviors, but they won't continue unless adults reinforce those behaviors.
Children with disabilities take up all of the caregiver's time, leaving little for the other children.	It's true that some children with disabilities require more attention from adults, but good planning can help children with disabilities become more independent and take less of the caregiver's time.
Children with disabilities have behavior problems.	Children with disabilities are no more likely to have behavior problems than are other children.
Some children have too many disabilities to get along well in an inclusive program.	Many children with severe disabilities have successfully participated in inclusive child-care settings.
Other children will make fun of children with disabilities.	Young children may have questions about a child's disability, but they rarely make fun. In fact, children view a child with disabilities as just another kid.

Inclusive child-care settings are good for parents, too. Parents of children with disabilities want their children to have the same opportunities as other children and to be a part of community life. Inclusive child-care settings give people with different abilities the chance to get to know one another, to appreciate what each has to offer, and to accept their differences. Parents with children in inclusive child-care settings learn a lot about how they can help their own children grow and develop.

Even you, the caregiver, benefit from an inclusive program. When you care for children with disabilities, you will learn new teaching skills that you will find useful with all the children you care for—and you'll be making a big difference in children's lives.

Goals of Inclusive Child-Care Settings

Until 1986, the laws addressed the education of *school-aged* children with disabilities, mostly ages 5 to 21. But our new laws encourage states to serve very young children, beginning at birth. Child-care settings that include children with disabilities have six important goals.

1. To help children develop in all areas. If you've ever listened to parents talking to one another, you've noticed that they often talk about what their children can do—who's spoken his first word, who's taken her first steps, who can count to ten, who's drawing pictures, who's learned to tie her shoes, and so forth. These parents are all talking about their child's *development.* There are five areas of development:

- *communication*—talking and listening
- *cognitive*—learning and thinking
- *adaptive*—taking care of one's self
- *social or emotional*—relating to people and developing a positive opinion of one's self
- *physical*—developing one's senses (seeing, hearing, touching, tasting, and smelling) and using the big muscles that move one's body and the little muscles that move one's fingers and hands

Caregivers plan activities that help children develop in each of the five areas. When you care for children with disabilities, you will need to pay particular attention to each child's development in each area because disabilities can interfere with the order in which skills are learned and the way in which skills are used.

2. To build acceptance for children with disabilities. By caring for children with and without disabilities together in the same setting, adults and children learn to understand and value each other's differences. This understanding leads to opportunities for developing friendships and helps children with disabilities become a part of the world of young children. When children are cared for together, they learn the social skills they need in order to get along in the world, such as speaking when spoken to, sharing, taking turns, using good table manners, and playing. Sometimes children with disabilities need extra help in learning how to play.

3. To help children regularly use the skills they've learned in many different situations. Have you ever taught a child to do something, like tie his shoes, and found out later that he will tie his shoes only in the child-care setting but never at home? This is a common problem in many programs that teach children with disabilities. They use the skills they learn in one setting *only in that place*—nowhere else! You can help children learn to use their skills in many different settings— at home, in the grocery store, or at Grandma's. Skills learned at one time of the day need to be practiced at other times of the day. In this way, children start using new skills regularly.

4. To support families of children with disabilities. Having a child with a disability puts extra demands on a family. When you care for one or more children with disabilities in your child-care setting, you help families meet and support each other. They see the ways their children are like other children. When children with disabilities are included in child-care settings, their families learn that they, like other families, can find and use quality care. Such programs help make sure that having a child with a disability doesn't keep families from doing the things that other families can do.

5. To help prevent future problems. A child with a disabilitiy can develop additional problems because of the disability. For example, a child who cannot talk might try to get attention by banging his head. Caregivers can prevent this problem by teaching the child better ways to get an adult's attention. Children who are used to having other people do a lot of things for them can become dependent and stop trying to do things for themselves. Caregivers can look one step ahead to make sure disabilities don't become bigger problems than they have to be.

6. To help children become more independent. Some people think that people with disabilities are helpless and need to have everything done for them. This is simply not true. What *is* true is that most children with disabilities can learn to take care of themselves and do many of the things that people without disabilities can do. Caregivers help children with disabilities along the road to independence by adapting materials and equipment, by teaching new ways to do a task, and by patiently encouraging children to do tasks independently when they are ready.

You're Part of a Team

Many children with disabilities receive special services either in the child-care setting or in a special program. Specially trained professionals help a child develop needed skills through therapy or special activities. These professionals often serve together with a child's parents' on a team, focusing on a child's needs. As a caregiver of a child with disabilities, you are part of this team. A team may be made up of as few as two people or many more. The team's job is to put together a plan for helping the child develop and learn and to help put that plan into action. Each team member has important knowledge about the child and the child's development. For example, a speech therapist can help plan the best ways to encourage the child's language development. As the caregiver, you will give the team information about the child's progress and your opinions about the child's needs. The team is important for children with disabilities because some children have needs that require the attention of specially trained individuals.

Who Are the Members of the Team?

The team might include any of the following people:

- *The family.* The child's parents, guardians, or foster parents are almost always part of the team. Sometimes, a person who is specially trained to watch over the special needs of the child is also a part of the team. This person is known as a *parent advocate* or *child advocate.* The family helps the team understand the child's needs and progress toward goals. In many cases, the parents are the ones who call a meeting to discuss a change in services or contact professionals who can address the needs of their child.

- *Preschool special educators or early intervention specialists.* Specialists have been trained to help children with disabilities. With the child's parents' and your permission, they might visit your day-care home or child-care center and give you tips on how to help the child learn and develop. They will also help you include the child in the activities of your child-care setting.

    As a member of the team, the special educator will help identify ways to meet the goals the team sets for the child and ways to decide whether or not goals are met. Later, he or she can help you put those strategies into action in the child-care setting.

- *Speech and language pathologist.* A speech and language pathologist is a person who has received special training to help children learn to communicate. He or she works on *speech,* or how well a child says words, and on *language,* or how a child uses words and sentences to say what is on his or her mind or to understand what others are saying. Speech and language pathologists also know a great deal about hearing and about how the face and mouth muscles work.

The speech and language pathologist helps identify goals related to the child's language development and ways to meet those goals. A speech and language pathologist may come to your child-care setting to work with a child and give you ideas about how to encourage language, or a child may go to an office or clinic to receive services.

- *Audiologist.* An audiologist tests children's hearing and finds the right kind of hearing aid for a child. An audiologist will advise the child's parents on how to help the child use and care for the hearing aid. You will need to ask the parents to share that information with you.

- *Physical therapist.* A physical therapist works with a child on learning to move large muscles, which may help the child learn to sit or walk. Physical therapists can help you learn the best ways to *position* a child who cannot sit, stand, crawl, or walk. To position a child means to place a child so that he or she is sitting or lying down on mats on the floor or in special equipment with the muscles situated in ways that allow them to strengthen and grow.

  Another important job of the physical therapist is to help families design or select special equipment to meet the needs of a child with physical disabilities. Such equipment might help a child get about independently (wheelchairs, walkers, carts), provide support for sitting or standing, or otherwise enable a child to participate in activities.

- *Occupational therapist.* Whereas the physical therapist helps a child learn to use large muscles, an occupational therapist helps a child learn to use the smaller muscles in hands and fingers. Smaller muscles are especially important in doing such things as feeding oneself, dressing, or combing hair. An occupational therapist can help you teach a child how to hold a spoon or crayon or learn to button buttons or string beads.

- *Health care provider.* A child's health care is an important part of his development. A nurse or doctor may be part of the team to make sure that the child's medical needs are met, particularly if a child has any chronic health problems.

■ *Service coordinator or team leader.* The service coordinator or team leader has administrative responsibilities, such as completing paperwork. This person helps to coordinate the special services for a child and also thinks about the needs of the child's family members.

On some teams, all of the team members listed above work together to set goals for each child's development and plan the special help a child will need. One member of the team may be chosen as the service coordinator to work with the child, the family, and the child-care provider, with help from other team members as needed.

■ *Caregiver.* You are the caregiver—the person who sees the child almost every day. You know a great deal about the child. You see how he or she behaves in a group of children. You know what the child can do, what she can't do, what she likes. Because you know the child better than perhaps anyone except the child's family, you are a very valuable member of the team. As a member of that team, you, too, can help identify goals and strategies for meeting them. You will give important information about the child's progress toward those goals. And although you may be the main person on whom the team relies to put many of the strategies into action, you will have the support of every other member of the team!

What Are the Responsibilities of the Team?

The team has four major responsibilities:

■ *Gather information.* The first job of the team is to gather information about the child. Each team member will help the team learn about the child. The family can help the rest of the team know what a child can already do. The speech and language pathologist will find out how well the child communicates. The physical or occupational therapist will help the team learn more about the child's muscle development. Team members may test the child to get the information they need; they may also watch the child playing or interview people who know the child well. After all the information is gathered, the team members share their information at a team meeting and identify the abilities and needs of the child.

■ *Decide which services are needed.* The second task of the team is to decide what services will meet the needs of the child. Together, the team members choose the goals for the child and write them into a

plan. The plan is designed to help families reach the goals they want for their children and is based on family priorities. For children under three years old, this plan is called the Individual Family Service Plan (IFSP). For children who are older than three, the plan is called the Individualized Education Program (IEP). These plans contain the goals that have been set by the team and strategies for meeting each goal. You can use the IFSP or IEP when you plan activities and a schedule for each child.

- *Coordinate services.* The third task of the team is to deliver services. With so many people focusing on one child, it is important to coordinate the services a child receives. Sometimes, there are so many services that a family may feel that all they do centers around services for the child. Families need time just to be families together. Many teams choose one person to do the work of the team together with the family, calling on other team members for help when needed.

- *Find out if the child is making progress.* The fourth task of the team is to find out if a child is making progress. Usually, members informally check in with one another about a child's progress. But every six months or so, team members will measure a child's progress in a more formal way, perhaps by testing or observing.

Working with the Team

Children with disabilities have many different needs, needs that may require special attention from a number of professionals. As the caregiver, you see the child as no one else does. It is important that you tell members of the team if you think that they are on the wrong track or if you feel something won't work. If you don't understand something, ask questions!

The other team members who work with a child may come to your child-care setting to provide services and to talk to you about how to help that child. Sometimes, however, specialists are not able to leave their offices or clinics to visit the child-care setting. When you have questions or concerns that you would like to share with other team members, be sure to let the family know so that they can decide how information can be shared.

Here's how one caregiver felt about being on a team.

At first, I felt a little uncomfortable in the team meetings. Everyone there seemed to know each other except me. They were using words I'd never heard. But soon I realized that they were talking about kids, and if there's one thing I know, it's kids. So I decided to speak up and say, "Just a minute, please. Before you go on, could you tell me what a thus-and-such is?" Most of the time, the word they used was just their jargon for something I already knew about. I don't know what happened—perhaps they stopped using the words, or perhaps I learned what they meant—but eventually, I understood what they were talking about and I began to feel like a real member of the team. I realized that they needed me and that I had a responsibility to the child with disabilities in my care. There were things I knew about her that they needed to know. For example, when I mentioned that Beth, who has cerebral palsy and has trouble controlling her arms, loved soft objects, the team (me included) decided that she might work really hard to use her arms if it meant getting hold of a stuffed animal. If I've learned anything about being a member of the team, it's to speak up!

Involving Parents and Families

A child's parents can provide you and other people involved in their child's care with valuable information that will help you set goals for the child and make day-to-day decisions. But parents also need support and information. Many inclusive child-care settings arrange parent gatherings that allow parents to mingle and share ideas. Others provide workshops and speakers to talk about topics of interest. But the most important part of involving parents is through friendly talks every day. Finding time each day to share a little information about the child with the parents can be hard, but these ideas can help:

- Write the parent a note about an activity the child did. Tell how the child acted and what the child may have said.
- Telephone the parent to share good news or tell about an activity the child especially enjoyed.

- Send home a newsletter telling about an activity enjoyed by many children and how the activity might be done at home.
- When sending home artwork, put the child's name and the date on it. Write a sentence that will help the parent talk about it with the child. You might write down what the child said about the picture and the materials that were used to create it.
- Ask parents to bring in supplies for special activities. Tell how and when the supplies will be used so that the parent has an idea of the activities going on in the child-care setting.
- Ask for the parents' advice and opinions whenever you set new goals for the child.

When You Are Concerned About the Development of Children

If you are worried about the development of a child in your care who is not receiving special services, first discuss your concerns with the family and let them know where they can get more information. In most states, children who are three years old can get a free evaluation through their local school system. The best way to find out where to get an evaluation for younger children is to ask local school system officials, the mental health center, the health department, or the child's pediatrician.

Getting to Know Children with Disabilities

KEY POINTS

■ All children develop at different rates.

■ Children who are developing typically reach developmental milestones in the same order and at about the same time as other children.

■ Disabilities affect the child's rate of development and the order in which developmental milestones are reached.

■ A diagnosis tells you something about a child's disability but does not tell you what a child can do or how much a child can learn in a lifetime.

What Is "Typical" Development?

It goes without saying that each child, with or without a disability, is very different from the next. In your child-care setting, you have some children who are moving all of the time and others who are content to sit quietly. You have children who are always telling you something and others who say very little. Some children would choose to spend their whole day in the block center; others can't get enough of the dress-ups. Some children are almost always happy, and others are much harder to please. You are sure to have noticed that children come in different sizes, even when they are the same age. Can all of these children be developing typically? The answer is yes!

Typical development means that children reach developmental milestones in the same order and at about the same time as other children. We can predict how most children will develop. We know that most children will develop certain skills—called *developmental milestones*—such as cooing, grasping a toy, crawling, and sitting alone—at roughly the same age. We also know that children will reach these skills in order. For example, all children learn to hold up their heads, roll over, and sit without support—*in that order*. Typical development occurs when children reach developmental milestones at certain times in their lives and in a certain order.

The *Baby Can, Ones Can, Twos Can,* and *Threes Can* lists in the Active Learning Series show skills that most children can learn to do within the same time span. However, you will find that each child will gain skills at his or her own rate, and that what one child can do will be different from what another child can do. Typically developing children are more likely to learn the skills on the lists at an even rate and at approximately the expected age. Children with disabilities are likely to learn at a less even rate and may have gaps in skill development. Although the *Can* lists might help alert you to a child whose development is not progressing as expected, the lists cannot be used to diagnose a disability. The *Can* lists are meant only to help you find out what the children are doing so that you can select appropriate activities.

Children develop at their own rates. Although children reach developmental milestones at fairly predictable ages and in a fairly predictable order, children still develop according to their own schedules. Some children develop fast, and others take their time. For example, one child may walk at eight months, but another may not walk until much later, at maybe 15 or 16 months—and both children are developing normally. Some children skip developmental milestones, like the child who never crawls but goes straight from standing alone to walking. Typically developing children are very different from each other, although their patterns of development are very similar.

What Are Disabilities?

Disabilities are characteristics of children that interfere with typical development. Disabilities may make it harder for children to reach certain developmental milestones or show that they have reached those milestones. Disabilities can affect a child's cognitive, physical, communication, adaptive, and social or emotional development. Although the disability might be in just one area, the disability may also affect a child's development in other areas. For example, if a child has a communication disability, he may also have problems learning about his world (because he may not understand what he is being told) or socializing (because he may not be able to talk with other children).

Scott was big, healthy, and handsome when he was born. But when it was time for Scott and his mother to go home from the hospital where he was born, Scott still hadn't learned to nurse and had a very weak sucking reflex. He was stiff to hold and didn't like to be cuddled. Even when he was taking a bottle or nursing, he would push away. As he grew older, he wasn't interested in toys and sometimes stared blankly as if he didn't see or hear. He walked at one year but never crawled.

At age two, when most children have begun to talk, Scott still did not communicate with either words or gestures. He became very upset with anything unfamiliar or unexpected—new noises, people, even a knock at the door. He was unable to entertain himself with toys or books, so he cried or fussed out of boredom when his mother or father wasn't entertaining him.

Scott's parents knew that their child was not developing typically and talked to their pediatrician about their concerns. The doctor asked about Scott's behavior and their family history. Based on that information, the doctor suggested testing at a local hospital. The tests confirmed that Scott had fragile X syndrome, a condition that can cause mental retardation and other learning problems, and that his development was delayed in all areas.

Even before Scott's parents learned the diagnosis, they had begun to look for a child-care setting that could meet Scott's needs. They felt that Scott should be in a program with typically developing children, but realized that the caregivers would need to be able to accommodate Scott's special needs. Later that year, at age two and a half, Scott was enrolled in a half-day program. Together, Scott's parents, caregivers, doctors, and other specialists worked to help Scott develop in all areas. By the time Scott turned four years old, he was understanding simple commands such as "no," "stop," "come here," and "give me" and could use a few words to express his needs. He could grasp a crayon with his whole fist and scribble happily on a piece of paper. Scott was ready to be toilet trained. Although changes in routines were still difficult for him, with an adult's careful planning, Scott could handle them.

Sometimes we know that a child has a disability at birth because the child is physically different from other babies, for example, when a child is born without fingers. Most disabilities are not as easily spotted, such as when a baby is born deaf. Disabilities may be the result of something that happened before, during, or after birth, and the cause is often unknown.

People use many different words to refer to people with disabilities, such as *handicapped, impaired,* and *exceptional.* You have probably heard other words, such as *mental retardation, learning disabled,* and *cerebral palsied.* When speaking about people with disabilities, it is important to remember that they are people first. For this reason it is more appropriate to say a *girl with disabilities* rather than a *disabled girl,* or to say a *boy with mental retardation* rather than a *mentally retarded boy.*

Spotting a Disability

Sometimes a doctor is the first to spot a child's disability, but often it is the child's parents or caregivers who first think that something is not quite right. The first sign an adult has that a child is not developing typically is that a child fails to reach developmental milestones at expected ages. For example, parents watch for children to startle at loud noises or to turn toward noises. If a child does not seem to hear noises in the way an adult expects, this is a signal that something might be wrong. Usually parents tell their concerns to a doctor. Sometimes the doctor will have a specialist examine the baby and do some tests. But other times, the doctor wants to wait and see if the child outgrows the problem. Sometimes parents and caregivers must insist before professionals agree that the child is having difficulty. A child with disabilities may see many specialists before a decision is made about whether the child has a disability, and if so, what the disability is. Once all the information is gathered, a specialist may be able to make a *diagnosis,* or tell what the child's disability is.

What Does a Diagnosis Tell You?

A diagnosis tells you something about a child, but not everything. The diagnosis will often tell you what kind of disability a child has, such as cerebral palsy, mental retardation, or deafness. The diagnosis will sometimes also tell you if the child's disability is *mild, moderate,* or *severe.* For example, consider children with hearing loss. A child who has mild hearing loss may get along just fine without a hearing aid and may learn to talk and read with very little trouble. A child with moderate hearing loss may need to wear hearing aids and receive speech and language therapy in order to learn to talk. A child with severe hearing loss may not be helped at all by wearing a hearing aid and may never learn to talk, but may learn to communicate using sign language.

Children with disabilities are as different from one another as children who are developing typically. Children with the same diagnosis can be very different from each other, just as children who are developing typically may be very different from each other. You may find that of two children who are diagnosed with moderate hearing losses, one picks up language much more quickly than the other. Or you may discover that one child with mental retardation is very outgoing and another is shy.

A diagnosis does not tell you how much a child will learn to do in his or her lifetime. Although some specialists will try to predict when a child will learn to walk, talk, or read, these predictions are often made too early to be accurate. A child's early experiences make a real difference in what is learned, and although each child has his or her limits, no one can be sure of exactly what they will be.

A diagnosis tells you...	A diagnosis does *not* tell you...
the type of disability a child has	how much the child will learn during his or her lifetime
whether the disability is mild, moderate, or severe	the activities that will help a child learn

Types of Disabilities

Disabilities can occur in any area of development but almost always affect development in other areas as well. It is important to remember that disabilities can be mild, moderate, or severe. Some children have *multiple disabilities,* or disabilities that appear in combination with other disabilities. The words *developmentally delayed* are sometimes used to describe children whose skills are below what is expected for their age.

Cognitive Disabilities

Children who have cognitive disabilities are often said to have mental retardation, mental disabilities, brain injury, or developmental delays. Children with Down syndrome have cognitive disabilities. Children with cognitive disabilities are slower than most children to reach the milestones in *all* developmental areas. The order in which they reach the developmental milestones is the same as for typically developing children, but children with cognitive disabilities take longer to get there. They may be slower to learn to walk, talk, and feed themselves.

It is generally harder for children with cognitive disabilities to learn new skills or to pay attention for long. You may notice that some children, especially those who have severe cognitive disabilities, don't notice what is going on around them and that you must work hard to get their attention.

Children with cognitive disabilities are very different from each other. Some children will be very loving; others may be in a world of their own. Some children will catch on to new tasks much more quickly than others. Each child will have different strengths and needs.

Richard, who has Down syndrome, came to our program when he was eighteen months old. He could sit by himself and was just learning to walk. Although Richard didn't use many words, he was very sociable. He liked to give hugs, wave bye-bye, and enjoyed being around other children. Even though Richard's development was behind other children's, he could participate in his own way in many of the activities for one-year-olds in the Active Learning Series. When he couldn't, I made sure that he was part of the action by adapting the activity. For example, one day we did an activity called "Riding Toy Music." We tied pull toys that made sounds to the back of riding toys so children could ride and listen at the same time. Richard couldn't ride a toy by himself, so I pulled him in a wagon to which we had tied a xylophone.

I noticed that it often took Richard extra time to catch on to an

---

Active Learning for Children with Disabilities

activity. Sometimes, I would do an activity where I would hide toys and let the children find them. Richard could not find a hidden toy if it was fully covered, but if I let a little bit of it show from its hiding place, he could.

In many ways, Richard was just like the other children in the group but just took longer to learn. When we counted together, it took Richard much more time to be able to say "one, two!" by himself. We counted two of just about everything—leaves, pegs, dolls, doorknobs. Richard, like most toddlers, would have gotten bored if we had only counted pegs, but because we counted many different things, he didn't get bored, but instead felt very proud of himself when he did it. I found that repeating activities wasn't a problem as long as we changed the materials we used and the settings in which we did the activity.

Physical Disabilities

Children with physical disabilities may have trouble controlling their muscles or may not be able to use their arms or legs at all. Sometimes, physical disabilities are called *orthopedic impairments* or *motor disabilities*. Cerebral palsy, spina bifida, arthritis, and muscular dystrophy all cause physical disabilities.

Some children with orthopedic impairments may have missing or deformed arms or legs. Sometimes physical disabilities make it harder for children to talk because they have trouble controlling the muscles used for speech. Also, children with physical disabilities may have trouble learning because they cannot move around to explore all the things that other children play with.

Each child with a physical disability needs to be handled differently. Some children will be able to move about the room unaided; others will use wheelchairs or walkers. Children with severe physical disabilities may not be able to sit or stand alone and will have special equipment.

Physical and occupational therapists, professionals who specialize in how people use their muscles, give advice about handling a child with physical disabilities. They can help you learn how to use any equipment the child needs. Most often parents have special equipment at home, too, and can show you how to use it.

Shawanna is three years old and has cerebral palsy. Only one side of her body is affected. On that side, the muscles in her arm, leg, neck, trunk, and face are tight and stiff. Her affected leg looks shorter than her other leg, and she has trouble making it move the way she wants it to. Her shoulder is pulled down and she holds her arm close to her body. Her foot points downward. She has trouble balancing herself when she stands, walks, or sits.

Shawanna has learned to use the unaffected side of her body well. She can feed herself, paint, and create colorful scribble pictures. She is very smart and catches onto ideas quickly, but because the muscles in her face are affected, she has some trouble talking and she often drools. Because she has difficulty getting her hands to work together and her legs to walk, she hasn't been able to explore the world around her the way she would like to. This sometimes frustrates her, and she gets tired and wants to give up. Praise and encouragement help perk her up and keep trying.

Shawanna sometimes needs an adult's help to enter into play with other children. It takes her longer to get to the play area, and because her speech is affected, she has difficulty letting other children know she would like to play.

Visual Impairments

Children with visual impairments see very poorly or cannot see at all. Many children with visual impairments are said to be blind, but this does not always mean that they cannot see anything. Some children can see light and dark; others can see fuzzy shapes and know if something moves. Even with glasses, children with visual impairments cannot see well enough to learn by watching.

When children cannot see, they cannot learn by watching, which is the most important way people learn. They cannot see other children blow bubbles and then learn how to blow bubbles themselves. They may not know that a kitten has four legs, two ears, and whiskers until they have held a cat and explored its body. They may not know that a cat says "meow" because they have never seen a cat open its mouth and make that sound. Although a child who is blind may be smart, he or she may take much longer to learn words, ideas, and actions.

Visual impairments affect all areas of development. Children with visual impairments may be slower to learn to walk, run, and jump than other children. You are likely to see children who are blind rocking, swaying, or twisting for no obvious reason. Some children who are blind do not move around the room much.

If you care for a child with visual impairments, you will need to be very involved in the child's learning. Because you cannot show a child something, you will need to explore the object together with the child, talking to the child and helping him use his other senses, especially hearing and feeling, to learn about the world.

Jenna has a visual impairment. She wears glasses held on by a headstrap. Although the glasses help Jenna see better, she sees only what is in the center of her vision. When Jenna was a baby, her parents noticed that she was not attracted to the colorful mobiles they hung above her crib and that she did not imitate others. As she grew older she rocked her body in an unusual fashion and would sometimes flutter her fingers in front of her face. Even after her baby days, she was still exploring things by putting them into her mouth. After a series of tests, she was diagnosed with tunnel vision, a condition in which a child cannot see things on the sides without moving her head. What vision she did have was blurred. Glasses corrected the blurred vision, but the tunnel vision remained.

Jenna learned to walk late. When other children were running around in a large open space, Jenna stayed close to her mother. When she did walk, she took cautious, jerky steps. Jenna needed much practice in order to learn to string beads, put pegs in a pegboard, or fit objects together. But Jenna was quick to learn to talk. She listened intently and often imitated what she heard, but sometimes, even though she used the word, she did not know what it meant because she had not seen the object or action.

Hearing Loss

An audiologist will test a child to see how well he or she can hear. The audiologist will tell how much a child can hear and whether the hearing loss is mild, moderate, severe, or profound. Children who cannot hear at all or who can hear only very loud noises are *deaf.* Other children with hearing loss can hear more but still have great difficulty understanding what people say. Sometimes hearing aids will help children with hearing loss, but not always.

A child may be born with hearing loss, or it may develop later in life because of an illness or an injury. It is harder for children who were born with hearing loss to learn to talk than it is for children whose hearing loss occurred later. Children who are born with severe or profound hearing loss may never learn to talk so that others can understand them. For this reason, the parents, together with a speech-language pathologist, will help them learn another way of talking, usually by using sign language. There are several different kinds of sign language, and the speech-language pathologist, the audiologist, and the child's parents will decide which method is best for the child.

It is very important for children with hearing loss to have a speech-language pathologist to help them learn to communicate. You will work very closely with parents and other professionals to know how a child communicates best and to help each child develop communication skills.

Rodney's hearing loss was present at birth and was diagnosed when he was one year old. Rodney had been in day care since the age of three months. The caregiver in the daycare center noticed that Rodney often did not react like other children to the things going on around him. Although he would startle at loud noises, he did not turn toward softer noises the way other children did. At six months, Rodney cooed and made noises like the other children, but at one year, he did not use any words and did not respond when his name was called. The caregiver discussed her concerns with Rodney's parents, who had noticed many of the same behaviors. They decided to have Rodney's hearing tested.

The tests showed that Rodney had a moderate hearing loss and that hearing aids would help him. An audiologist fitted Rodney with hearing aids and discussed with Rodney's parents and caregiver the possibility of using sign language along with speech to help Rodney learn to communicate. Rodney's parents decided to learn sign language and the caregiver also learned a few important signs. Now, at age three, Rodney uses both signs and speech to communicate. His voice is high pitched and nasal, he mispronounces many words, and speaks in short sentences. The other children in the setting include Rodney in their play, but they often need help understanding what he is saying.

Except for talking clearly, Rodney can do most of the things the other children do. He likes to jump, climb, and ride the tricycle. He enjoys pounding clay and painting. He builds roads out of blocks for toy cars. Even though Rodney has hearing loss and communication difficulties, he is still able to participate fully in the activities.

Health Impairments

All children get sick, but they usually get well in a few days. Some children, however, have health problems that never go away. These are called chronic health problems. Some of the more common chronic health problems children have are *leukemia, cystic fibrosis, asthma, heart defects, sickle cell anemia, cancer,* and *diabetes.* Each of these diseases is very different from the other and must be treated by a doctor. Children who have these diseases can be mildly, moderately, or severely affected, and sometimes the condition is better and sometimes worse. Some children will even go into *remission* for a period of time and not seem sick at all.

Other children and adults will not catch the disease that the child has—the diseases are not contagious, but they do require special attention in the child-care setting. The child's doctor or nurse can help parents and caregivers learn how to best care for each child.

As a caregiver, you will notice that children with health impairments get tired very quickly. Some children will not feel like doing much; others will be cranky. Like most children who aren't feeling well, children with health impairments often need to be cuddled and comforted by an adult more often than other children to feel secure.

Because children with chronic health problems are sick or in the hospital often, they miss many chances to make friends. You can see how important inclusive child-care settings are for children with health impairments: being in a setting with other children their age will give them many chances to make friends.

Although children with health impairments may not have other disabilities, their development can still be affected. They often miss out on learning because they are sick. Children with health impairments might also learn to depend on others more than they really need to. For this reason, one goal for many children with health impairments is to help them learn to do everything they can for themselves.

Timmy is a three-year-old boy with cystic fibrosis. His body makes a sticky mucous in his lungs that must be coughed up so that he can breathe. Fortunately for Timmy, he has a mild case of cystic fibrosis and has been hospitalized only once in his life with pneumonia. He gets tired easily, especially when on the playground, and active play makes him cough harder and more often. Coughing is good for Timmy because it keeps his lungs clear, so the caregivers encourage him to run and play with the other children.

Timmy can easily participate in all the activities going on in the child care setting, although he likes quiet activities more than active ones. He talks about his thoughts and ideas well and is gaining skills at about the same rate as his peers. Except for making sure he gets lots of rest, the caregivers do not need to do any activities differently to include Timmy.

Behavior Problems

All children behave in ways you wish they wouldn't every now and then. It's part of the way children learn about what is right and wrong and how to behave in certain situations. With adult guidance, most children will learn from these experiences and will try to behave appropriately most of the time, although they won't always be successful. Most children go through stages when they are picky eaters, have fears, throw temper tantrums, fight, want to be alone, or are very active. It is when these problems stay around for a very long time and interfere with a child's development that the child is said to have behavior problems.

Severe behavior problems in very young children are rare. Strategies for handling behavior problems are discussed in the *Planning* section of the Active Learning Series and are useful tools for helping all children learn to behave appropriately. If a child with severe behavior problems is in your group, you may want to seek advice from a specialist in this area.

Sometimes children with other disabilities develop behavior problems. For example, children who are unable to use words may get very frustrated and, as a result, throw temper tantrums. In fact, it is likely that many undesirable behaviors—such as grabbing, biting, and throwing—are actually ways children communicate when they cannot use words. The child who grabs a toy may not be grabbing to be mean or annoying, but because he or she wants attention, affection, help, or the toy itself and doesn't know how to use words to get it.

Speech and Language Disabilities

Speech and language are two different, but related, abilities that have to do with a person's ability to communicate. If you say that someone's *speech* is good, you are saying that he or she says (or *articulates*) words correctly and clearly. Language, on the other hand, refers to how someone puts words and sentences together to get across a thought or idea or how a child understands what someone else is saying.

All children make mistakes in the way they say words, and adults enjoy hearing the cute ways that children say things. Gradually, most children become able to say words correctly by six or eight years of age. Just because a preschooler doesn't pronounce words clearly doesn't mean he or she has a speech disability. Concern arises when children continue to say words that others cannot understand. They may stutter or put many unnecessary sounds in their speech. Children with speech problems are usually developing normally in other areas, but sometimes a speech problem is just a sign that a child is having other developmental problems. Children with speech problems may behave inappropriately because they cannot get others to understand what they are saying. If a child with a speech problem asks for a turn on the seesaw but isn't understood by the other children, she might push a child off to make room for herself.

A language disability is a different type of problem. A child may be able to say words clearly but may not be able to put words together to say what he wants to say. This child may also have trouble understanding what others say. Most children with cognitive disabilities or hearing impairments are slow to develop language skills.

Children who have trouble communicating may have trouble learning because they can't understand what is being talked about. They may also have difficulty making friends because friendship depends on communication. A child who cannot tell you what he wants or feels will be frustrated and may develop behavior problems. Talking with children as you do the activities in the Active Learning Series helps children develop communication skills.

Causes of Disabilities

Many disabilities are present in a child at birth, even though they may not be seen until much later. Sometimes disabilities are *inherited*, or passed down from the mother or the father to the child. Others are caused when something goes wrong in the cells as the baby is developing.

Illnesses and accidents can also cause disabilities. High fevers for long periods of time can affect a child's hearing. Other diseases can affect the brain, causing a typical child to have a cognitive disability. Accidents—such as car crashes, falls, burns, and poisoning—can also injure a child and cause a disability.

The care and attention a child gets in his or her home greatly affects a child's development. If a child lives in a home where no one pays any attention to her or where she must spend a lot of time alone, she will not learn the things she needs to learn at the right times. Children learn best in homes in which adults talk to, play with, and care for them and provide a variety of books and toys for children's play.

Many times, despite many tests, we simply are not able to learn what has caused a disability. Many families decide to stop their search for a cause and decide instead to search for the best ways to care for and teach the child and to show the child that he or she is a loved and valued family member.

Extra Help for Children with Disabilities

Disabilities always make it more difficult for a child to learn on her own. A child with disabilities will need some extra help from his or her parents, caregivers, and other professionals.

- *Children with disabilities may need more help.* A child with a disability may need to be helped, guided, or encouraged to do things. For example, a three-year-old child with a physical disability may need to be fed by an adult, or a child who is blind may need to be encouraged to explore different areas of the room. A child-care provider will give children the help they need but will also work with them to achieve independence.

- *Children with disabilities may need encouragement to become independent.* Although it is very important to give children with disabilities the help they need, it is just as important *not* to give them help they *don't* need. Children who have everything done for them whether they need it or not will not learn to be independent. Helping a child become independent takes a lot of patience from parents and caregivers, because it is sometimes easier to do it yourself than it is to teach or wait for a child to do it alone. So, for example, the adult will help the child feed himself or herself a few bites and gradually teach the child how to take over.

- *Children with disabilities may need help learning to relate to people.* All young children need help learning how to play together. They usually make friends as they play side by side. But children with disabilities may not have had the chance to play alongside other children because of physical problems or may not notice that other children are around. The children may need help to become aware of the people and activities going on around them and understand how to enter into play activities. Caregivers can help the child with disabilities learn how to be included in play and how to invite other children to be part of his play.

No one knows how far a child with disabilities can go, but we do know that with the right early experiences, children have a better chance to reach their full potential. Remember what the child *can do* rather than what he can't do. This will help you use the child's strengths to help him grow and develop.

Adapting the Child-Care Environment

KEY POINTS

- The child-care environment includes indoor and outdoor spaces, the schedule of activities, the toys and materials in the setting, and most important, the adults who talk and play with children.

- A good child-care environment has spaces for different kinds of play.

- Keeping spaces clean and safe is important to the health and well-being of both children and adults.

- Play spaces and activities may need to be adapted to meet the needs of children with disabilities, and planning ahead is important.

- Dependable routines and schedules help children feel safe.

To many people, the word *environment* means the air, earth, water, and living things around us. A child's environment, whether at home or in child care, is all these things and more. It is the air children breathe and the surfaces they walk or crawl on; it is the room they play in and the setup of the toys and furniture in the room and on the playground; it is also things you cannot see or touch, such as the daily schedule and the activities. The most important feature of the child-care environment is the way adults talk and play with children because these can create a feeling of warmth and enthusiasm or cool detachment.

The child-care environment includes

- the adults who talk and play with children
- indoor and outdoor spaces
- the schedule of activities
- the toys, books, and other learning and playing materials in the room

The difference between a poor child-care setting and a great one is the quality of the environment. The equipment in the child-care setting, how it is arranged, and what child-care providers do to help children use the things in the child-care setting make a big difference in what children learn during the day.

Quality child-care environments for young children

- are predictable—children know what to expect
- are responsive—adults play and talk with children; the toys and other materials are interesting to children and easy for them to use
- are safe and comfortable
- have separate spaces for different kinds of activities
- encourage children to explore and learn by doing

Indoors and Outdoors

Using Spaces to Help Children Learn

Environments affect how people act and feel. Think about the difference between a fast-food restaurant and a more formal restaurant where your order is taken and food is brought to your table. In the fast-food restaurant, the space is arranged so that people can wait in line at a counter to order and help themselves to napkins and straws. At a more formal restaurant, there is no counter or self-serve stand because people are expected to sit down and be served. In this environment, you would never think of getting up to get your own food or napkin.

Just like different kinds of restaurants, well-planned child care environments encourage children to act in certain ways. For example, if a room has large open spaces, children will tend to run, fight, and not take part in quiet play. If that same space is separated into smaller sections with no large open spaces or runways, children are more likely to play quietly in small groups. This is why good early childhood environments divide a large space into activity areas or interest centers. These are small spaces in a room where all the space, materials, and furnishings for one type of activity are provided. Examples of activity areas include an art space, block corner, and housekeeping center. These are spaces where children can take out, use, and put away all they need for an activity without having to leave the area.

The Active Learning Series has suggestions for setting up spaces both indoors and outdoors for various age groups and different kinds of play. The series suggests activity centers that children of certain ages will enjoy and gives ideas for toys and furnishings for those spaces (see *Materials and Notes* given for each type of activity). The information given under the heading *Activity Checklist* suggests ways to present and carry out activities so that they are safe and fun for everyone.

When a large space is clearly divided into activity centers, children soon learn what they are to do in each space because of the way it looks and the things that are in it. They find that certain spaces are for quiet activities, such as reading books or listening to tapes. When a child enters that space, he or she can tell that it is a place for quiet play because it may be tucked away in a corner away from noisier activities, it may contain a rug and pillows, and it may be big enough for only two or three children at a time. Other spaces that are for more active play are usually larger so that more children can play together in the space. Examples of noisy spaces are the block corner with toy cars and trucks and the housekeeping corner set up for dramatic play.

When a large space is divided into activity areas, some children can do quiet activities without being distracted. Others can get the benefits of more active play without disrupting the whole room. Best of all, the adults can let the space arrangement work to guide the behavior of the children.

Using Boundaries to Separate Play Spaces

There are many ways to divide a large room into smaller spaces. The easiest and most useful way is to use bookcases and storage units. Then you will have plenty of shelves to store the things children use as they play. You can also build moveable carpeted risers (which children can also climb on) to separate play spaces. Build them in L or U shapes so that children using wheelchairs or walkers can go around the risers to get in and out of the play space easily. They

should measure about 12 inches high and at least 12 inches deep. These lower dividers are great for dividing play spaces for babies. For older children, they do not separate noisy and quiet activities very well, but they are good if you want to divide a large space into two smaller spaces with similar activities. For example, a large block center might be divided in half with risers. Remember that you want the freedom to change the space as the children's needs change.

You can also use color to divide spaces. Paint the walls, shelves, tables, and other furnishings all the same color to signal the beginning and end of a particular space. You will still need real dividers, such as bookcases, but using colors gives children more clues to what goes together in the room.

Planning for Different Types of Play Spaces

A good environment for young children should have separate play spaces that focus on a kind of play that will help children grow in one or more of the major areas of development. But we should not let play spaces limit what the child can learn. Although we may set up an area to encourage one type of skill, it's important to remember that children are always working on lots of skills at one time. So while you encourage one skill, it also helps to encourage others, too. No matter what activities you are doing with the children, you can help them develop in several different areas at once. For example, playground equipment helps children develop physical skills, but at the same time they can learn language if you talk with them about what they are doing. "You are swinging high!" "One-two-three—now jump!" Whatever children are doing, you will help them develop their language skills by talking and asking questions.

Play spaces that help children develop their large muscles.
The environment should include indoor and outdoor spaces so that children can use their large muscles.

Outdoor spaces might have
- lots of room to run without bumping into equipment or other children
- climbers with steps and ramps so that all children can use them
- several types of swings—tire swings for more than one child, swings with supports that help a child stay on, swings for those who can hold on and pump, some lower and some higher so that all can reach, maybe a special swing that will hold a wheelchair
- wheel toys—some with pedals and some without—plus wagons to pull and carts to push

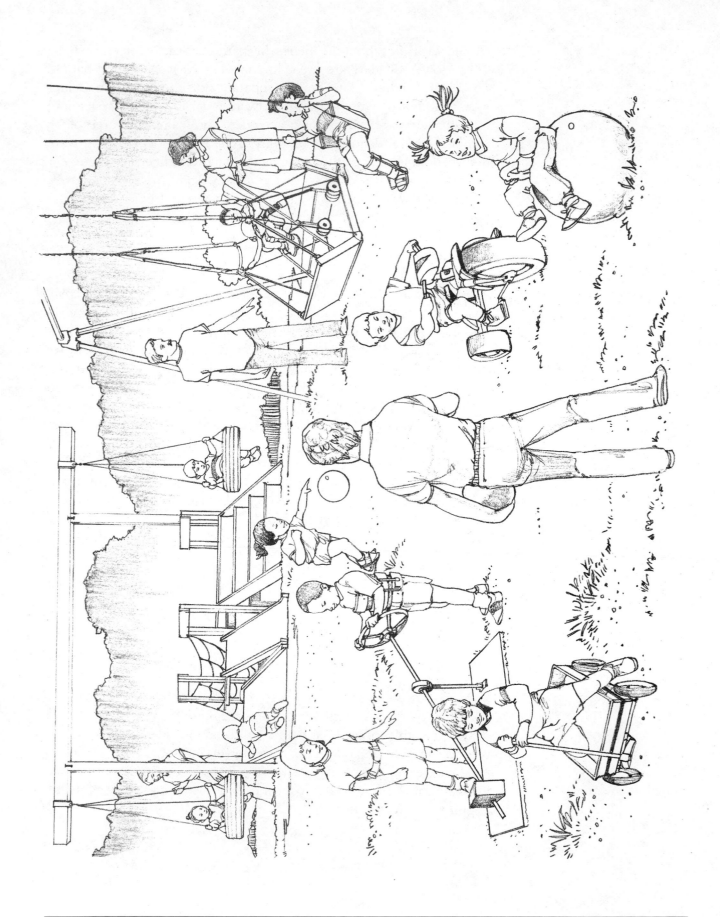

Indoor spaces might have

- a location where active play will not interfere with quiet play
- carpeted steps and ramps that lead to small slides
- large vinyl-covered foam mats to change the level of the floor with some interesting toys in different places on the mats
- low balance beams of different widths for different challenges
- low, small climbers
- mats under all climbers to cushion any falls
- large hollow wooden blocks
- some wheel toys to push, pull, or ride, if there's enough room

For babies, these spaces might contain

- cradle gyms
- rattles
- soft dolls
- a roll for propping baby
- small balls (ones that are too big for a baby to put in his mouth)

Play spaces that help children develop their smaller muscles. Small toys help children develop the small muscles in their hands and fingers. These things should be stored on a shelf where older children who will not put them in their mouths can easily reach them. An adult should watch closely while children play to make sure that they do not put small toys in their mouths. Space to use the toys should be next to the shelves, so that children do not have to carry toys with many pieces to a far-away play space. Pieces kept close to play areas are less likely to get lost. Spaces for small muscle development might contain low tables where children can sit on the floor and play at the table, a table with small chairs, or a rug to show where the play area is. Children are perfectly happy to play with toys on a comfortable carpeted area, and the pieces never fall out of reach.

Play spaces might have

- beads to string
- Legos™ or Duplos™
- easy puzzles
- pegboards
- jars with lids
- easy sewing cards
- little blocks and other little toys
- pull-apart beads
- activity boards with zippers, knobs, and dials
- fat crayons and paper
- large pegs and pegboards

For babies, these spaces might contain

- rattles
- large pull-apart beads
- a busy box

Spaces for listening and talking.

Set aside a space in the room for quiet play such as reading, resting, and listening to tapes that helps children develop many cognitive and language skills.

Quiet play spaces might contain

- beanbag chairs or lots of cushions
- picture books
- story tapes
- pictures or photos cut out and pasted onto sturdy cards and coated with clear contact paper

For babies, these spaces might contain

- hard-page books
- plastic-coated pictures
- design pictures

Spaces that encourage creative play.

Art and music, pretending, and playing with blocks help children learn as they create. You will probably want separate spaces for art, blocks, and pretend play. You don't need a separate space for music. Store some of the materials in activity boxes so that you can pull them out when you want to use them.

Choose a space for art that will be easy to clean up because some activities are messy. Store supplies on low shelves, so that older preschoolers can use them independently. Two-year-olds will need a more limited selection; toddlers will need an adult who can bring things out and supervise closely.

Stock the art space with

- paints and brushes
- crayons
- paste and white glue
- pipe cleaners
- many types of paper
- scissors (for both right-handed and left-handed children)
- clay and play dough

For babies, this space might have

- a patterned quilt or mat for baby to lie on and look at
- clear, bright pictures pasted on sturdy cards and coated with contact paper
- colorful mobiles
- design cards placed where babies can gaze at them while seated in baby seats

Spaces for pretending.
Pretending and acting out their own ideas help children develop communication skills, cognitive skills, and especially social or emotional skills. You might occasionally use a large refrigerator box to make a backdrop to suggest different themes for dramatic play, such as a storefront, garage, or circus for older children, or a house for toddlers.

Spaces for pretending might have

- dress-up clothes and hats
- real household items such as pots and pans and old telephones
- child-size tools and kitchen appliances
- dolls and large stuffed animals

For babies, this space might have

- plastic telephone
- hand puppets
- an unbreakable mirror

Spaces for block play might have

- lots of hardwood blocks
- smaller colored blocks
- small cars and animals
- dollhouse dolls
- colorful mats or cloths to play on and to use for roofs

For babies, block play might include

- cloth-covered foam blocks
- colorful wooden cubes (too big to be swallowed)
- plastic blocks that stick together when wet
- blocks with bells inside them
- blocks for sorting into containers

Materials for enjoying music might include
- musical instruments that children can bang or shake, such as bells, drums, and tambourines
- tape recorder with tapes
- music boxes
- lists of songs
- pictures of musical instruments

Spaces for learning about the world.

Some play spaces should be set aside for activities that teach children about their world. A center for sand and water play can help children learn about their world through their own discoveries. You might also have a center for learning about nature. Here children might watch an ant farm, place collections of fall leaves, or hold a pet. At other times, the center might contain materials for older children to sort by color, shape, or size. For babies, these spaces might contain an aquarium or fish bowl, stuffed animal toys, and nature mobiles.

A sand and water space might have
- a variety of pouring, sifting, and scooping toys
- sponges and corks of different sizes to learn what sinks and what floats
- individual dishpans for toddler sand and water play
- materials for sweeping sand and drying spills

Play Materials for Children with Disabilities

You probably already have many toys for the children in your care. Children with disabilities will be able to use many of these toys, but chances are you will need to buy or make some new ones and adapt others for use by children with certain types of disabilities. Children with motor disabilities will need toys that they can operate by using the skills they already have. Children with visual disabilities or hearing loss need toys that they can enjoy through their other senses. Children with cognitive disabilities need toys to play with at their developmental level that are also age-appropriate. You may also need to find toys that encourage development in a certain skill area.

Think about the toys you already have. You might want to make a list that will help you decide what kinds of new toys you might need. Start by listing the play spaces in your room across the top of the page, making a column for each space. Then go through the toys you have and write the name of the toy under the space where it belongs. Some toys could go in two or more areas. Note the areas in which you have enough toys and those that need more.

Next, consider the children with disabilities in your care and think about how each one can use the toys in each play space of the room. Taking each child one at a time, ask yourself the following questions:

- *Are the toys in this space safe for this child?* Consider safety when thinking about how the child is likely to use the toys. Is it likely that the toy would be used in such a way that it might hurt another child (if it is thrown, for example)? Is the toy made of nontoxic materials so that it will not hurt the child if it is mouthed? Is it washable? Are its parts large enough not to be swallowed? Does it have parts that stick out and may hurt a child?

- *Are the toys strong enough that they can't be easily broken?* Think about how the child with disabilities may use this toy, remembering that children with disabilities, especially those with behavioral problems, may use toys in ways they were not planned to be used.

- *Are there toys in the space that look "real"?* The more real a toy looks (dolls like real babies, pots and pans like the ones used in a real kitchen, pictures that look like the real thing), the more appealing it is to very young children. Usually, as children get a little older, they enjoy playing with toys that look less real because they can use their imaginations.

- *Do some of the toys in the space do something—make noises, produce flashing lights, talk, or move—when a child plays with them?* Children learn that their actions make something happen when they play with such toys. Toys that respond help children feel powerful and in control.

- *Are the toys attractive to both children and adults?* Because children learn best when adults play along with them, toys should be attractive to both age groups.

- *If the child has physical disabilities, are there toys in the space that the child can manage independently with his or her motor skills?* Such toys might need to be battery-operated with easy-to-turn switches.

- *If the child has visual disabilities or hearing loss, are there toys in the space that the child can enjoy using his or her other senses?*

- *If the child has cognitive disabilities, are there toys in the space that both he and typically developing children of the same age would all enjoy using?* Toys that can be used by children with differing skill levels are best, such as blocks, art materials, and pretend play toys.

- *Can the toys be easily cleaned to prevent illness being passed by the toys from one child to another?* This consideration is especially important for children with health impairments, who may be more likely to catch an infectious disease than other children.

- *Are there toys in the space that allow children of different developmental levels to play together?*

Making Environments Safe and Healthy

A good child-care environment considers the health and safety of the children. The Active Learning Series contains suggestions for keeping children in each age group safe (see *Making Spaces Safe and Healthy* sections in each book). Because the life experiences of children with disabilities may differ from those of typically developing children, you may find that the safety tips given for younger age groups pertain to some older children with disabilities, especially those with cognitive disabilities. Reading the safety tips for all age groups will remind you of precautions that will ensure the well-being of all the children in your care.

Children are more likely to get sick when they are cared for in group settings than if they are cared for at home because more people together means more germs. Although it is normal for children to get sick several times a year, good health practices will reduce the number of times children and adults get sick. Some children with disabilities are more likely to become sick than other children, so the importance of preventing illness through good health practices is even greater.

Disease is spread most often through body fluids such as mucous, blood, saliva, vomit, bowel stools, and urine. When a child with a cold wipes his nose with his hand (or even if he uses a tissue) and then picks up a toy, germs get on the toy. If another child picks up the toy later, that child may catch the cold. If a caregiver changes a diaper, then hands a toy to a child, germs from the diaper are transferred from the caregiver's hands to the toy and on to the child. You can see how important it is to wash your hands, as well as the children's, and to disinfect toys.

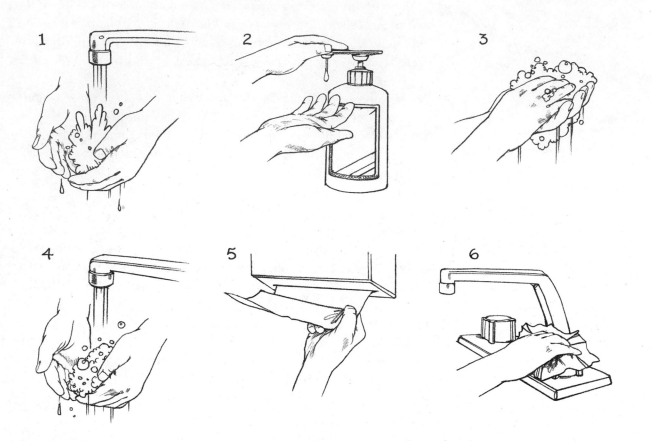

Hand-Washing Steps

Hand washing is the most important thing you can do to keep yourself and the children in your care healthy. As a caregiver, you will be washing your hands many times a day, so keep hand lotion ready! Follow these six steps.

1. *Always use warm running water.* Do not use a basin filled with water where germs can grow.
2. *Always use a liquid soap.*
3. *Rub hands together for at least 15 seconds to wash away germs.*
4. *Rinse off soap.*
5. *Dry hands.*
6. *Turn off the faucet with a paper towel.*

When to wash your hands

- When you come to work, before starting work with the children
- After changing a diaper, even if you use gloves
- After helping a child in the bathroom or using the bathroom yourself
- Before and after treating a child's cut, wound, or sore
- Before and after handling food
- Before and after feeding a child

- After cleaning up saliva (drool), blood, or vomit (even if you use gloves)
- After wiping your own or a child's nose or mouth
- Before and after giving a child medicine
- Before and after helping a child with a hearing aid, catheter, or other medical device
- After handling a toy that has been mouthed or otherwise come in contact with body fluids
- After handling pets or other animals or plants
- Whenever your hands are dirty

When to wash children's hands

- Before and after eating
- Before and after helping to prepare food or to set the table
- After a child uses the bathroom or has a diaper changed
- After a child wipes his or her nose or mouth
- Before and after handling his or her hearing aid, catheter, or other medical device
- After handling a toy that has been mouthed or otherwise come in contact with body fluids
- After handling pets or other animals or plants
- Whenever a child's hands are dirty

Disinfecting Toys and Equipment

All toys and equipment used with children need to be cleaned regularly. Purchase only toys that can be washed in the dishwasher, sink, or washing machine.

Every day

- Prepare a solution of bleach—1/4 cup bleach (no more) to one gallon of water. This solution should be kept away from children. This solution can be used to disinfect the diapering space, the tables where the children eat, and for washing down cribs, chairs, and other equipment. When it loses its chlorine smell—even if it has been prepared fresh in the morning—it is no longer good and should be thrown out and replaced.
- Set an empty basin on a high shelf. After a child has mouthed or otherwise infected a toy, toss it in the basin. Wash the toys at the end of the day in soapy water and air dry them.
- Fill a spray bottle with the bleach solution. Use the spray and paper towels to disinfect the diapering table after each use. Frequently spot clean tabletops, trays, countertops, handrails, toilet seats, bathroom walls, and other surfaces.
- At the end of the day, use the spray and paper towels to wipe down all the surfaces in the room, including those mentioned above. After wiping the surface free of food, dirt, or other

substances, spray on the disinfectant and let it air dry. When you are finished, pour the remaining spray down sinks and toilets to disinfect them.

- Wash bedding between uses if used by different children; wash when dirty even if used by only one child.
- Wash or vacuum floors.

At least once a week, but more often if needed

- Wash all stuffed animals in the washing machine.
- Wash all sheets and other bedding.
- Wash dress-up clothes.

Room Safety

Keeping the room safe for young children takes a lot of planning! Children who are crawling on the floor can find things that you may never see from up high. Take a child's-eye view of your room and ask yourself the following questions:

- Are all outlets covered with safety plugs?
- Are medications and cleaning supplies in locked storage out of reach?
- Are all the easily reached pieces of toys too big for babies to swallow? Are small toys that can be swallowed kept away from children who might put them in their mouths?
- When you are standing, can you quickly glance in each play space to monitor the activities of the children? Do you know where the hiding places are and are they safe places for children to be alone?
- Do platforms or lofts in the room have sturdy railings spaced close together so that children cannot fall through them, climb over them, or get their heads stuck?
- Can you reach any child who might need help in any space in the room?
- Is only unbreakable glass or plastic in children's spaces?
- Do drawers that contain knives, pins, needles, matches, and other dangerous things have childproof locks on them? Are they kept locked?
- Do you follow safety precautions when you cook, such as turning pot handles toward the back of the stove? Are stove knobs out of the reach of children? Is the place where you cook off limits to the children?
- Do hot radiators have covers over them?

Each book of the Active Learning Series contains an *Activity Checklist* before each set of activities. This checklist contains specific recommendations for making sure spaces are safe so that activities can be carried out without endangering children.

Making Spaces Accessible to Children with Disabilities

The room should allow all children, with or without disabilities, to explore fully the spaces, toys, and activities in it. The same is true for the playground. You may need to make changes in the room for children with disabilities. Most of the changes will probably be small ones that do not require you to spend a lot of money.

To know what changes to make, it might help if you pretend that you have the same disability the child has. For example, if the child uses a walker, go through the daily schedule maneuvering the walker yourself. Begin with arrival. Can you get from the parking lot or driveway into the room using the walker? Can you hang up your coat while using the walker? Can you freely move around furniture in the room? Can you get into the bathroom and to the toilet and sink? If you have a child with a visual impairment, walk through the room, paying attention to traffic patterns and obstacles at eye level, such as tabletops, shelves, drawers, cupboard doors, breadboards, and so on. Then walk through the room in the dark. After you have corrected all the problems you noticed, watch the child and note any problems he or she still has.

Remember that it is important for the child to be as independent as possible. If an adult must carry a child, reach toys, or move furniture so that the child can take part in daily activities, changes are needed. Ideas for adapting indoor and outdoor spaces for children with disabilities are given later in this chapter.

Adapting Spaces for Children with Disabilities

Basic room arrangement. For some children with disabilities, it is important to have things in the same place day after day. Children with visual impairments are free to explore and learn when a space is set up with clearly defined pathways and play areas. If you find that something is not working well, change the arrangement and then be sure to show all children how things have been changed.

Ramps. Children in wheelchairs or walkers need ramps where there are steps. Ramps can be bought or built. Make sure the ramp is not too steep—for each inch in height, the ramp should be one foot in length.

Coat hooks. Use coat hooks rather than hangers. Make sure coat hooks are within a child's reach, but not so low that they could poke a child's eye. Some coat hooks are easier to use than others, so visit your local hardware store to try them out before you buy. A large patch of Velcro might be easier than a coat hook for some children to use. Put a large square of the rough part on the wall and sew a large square of the soft part on the child's coat.

A child with a visual impairment will find her coat hook more easily if it is the first or last one in a row. You may want to mark that child's cubby or hook with a piece of fake fur or cotton so that he or she can easily find it by touching.

Tables. Children who crawl or scoot around the room need tables that are low to the ground. If your tables have adjustable legs, try them at their lowest height. Evenly saw off the legs of regular wooden tables so that they are the right height for children who spend their time on the floor. Children who are in wheelchairs may need tables that are a little higher than usual. If you care for children with different disabilities, you may need several tables of different heights.

Shelves. Most of the shelves in the room should be low and open. Take the doors off cabinets so that children can easily get to the toys inside. Make sure a variety of toys are available at each height so that children using wheelchairs and those who are crawlers will each be able to get interesting toys independently. Heavy things should be put as low as possible.

Children with visual disabilities need a way to find out what kind of material is on the shelves without handling everything. Strips of different textures, such as sandpaper, fake fur, vinyl, cotton, and so forth, can be glued to the ends or edges of shelves to indicate the type of item that is on the shelf or in a box. For example, a strip of fur on the outside of a storage box could indicate that dress-up clothes and hats are inside.

Make sure that shelves and cabinets cannot easily be pulled over if a child bumps into them or uses them for support. Although you may use low shelves to divide the room into activity spaces, make sure that they are far enough apart so that children using walkers and wheelchairs can easily get in and around them. You should be able to see over all of the shelves into the activity spaces to monitor the children.

Floors. Walkers, wheelchairs, and scooters may have a difficult time moving from vinyl or wooden floors to carpeting. Keep carpeted spaces, such as the book corner, near the walls of the room so that a child does not frequently have to travel across the carpet on his or her way to other activity spaces. Tape down the edges of all carpets to prevent tripping.

For children with visual impairments, it is particularly important to keep the floor free of unnecessary clutter. Put wastebaskets, boxes, and so forth under tables.

Changes in the way things feel can be signals to children with visual disabilities. If you have built carpeted risers as dividers for your room, cover them with carpets that have different textures. Children who are blind will connect the toys that are in a particular space with the texture of the carpet riser.

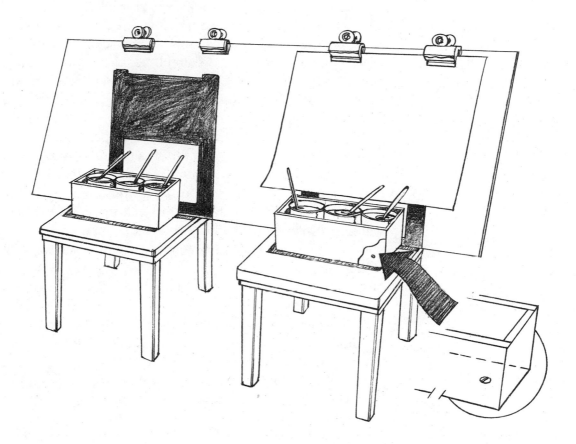

Easels. Instead of using easels that are easily knocked over, expensive, and take up a lot of room, try a sturdier solution, such as the following: Cover a large piece of plywood with plastic contact paper, or use plexiglass. Put an old chair with its back against the wall. Screw a plastic bin (the kind you put in kitchen drawers) at the front of the chair seat. Prop the plywood or plexiglass between the chair back and the plastic bin. Attach painting paper to the plywood with large clips. Put plastic jars of paint in the bin.

Bathroom. You may need to install grab rails near the toilet and sink to help children with disabilities become independent in the bathroom. Make sure children can easily reach the toilet paper, towels, and soap. It may be easier for some children to use liquid soap if the dispenser is attached to the wall. A large, open trash can is easier to use than a small one with a lid.

Children in wheelchairs may not be able to reach the sink. Although it is not recommended practice when children can get to a sink, you may need to put a wash basin and towels on a low table to be used only by children who are unable to get to a sink. It must be emptied and disinfected after each use.

Lighting. Good lighting is important for all children, but particularly for children with certain kinds of visual disabilities or hearing loss. Some children with visual disabilities can see better in bright light; for others bright light may be painful. Children with hearing loss need good light to see faces and gestures that help them understand what is being said. Track lights are inexpensive and easy to install to brighten up dim spaces.

Playground. Make changes on the playground to meet the needs of children with visual or physical disabilities. First you need to be sure that children can move around on the playground. The ground should be free of roots or other things that could trip a child. Pathways should be made of a material that allows wheelchairs and walkers to move freely while at the same time being soft enough for children to play on safely. With creativity, you can find cost-wise solutions to this problem. One caregiver covered sand paths with large rubber conveyor strips that had once been used at a rock quarry.

Look at your playground equipment with the child with disabilities in mind. It may be that you will need to mount the sandbox on a table so that a child can get to it.

You might cut a notch in the table to help a child with poor balance to stand. There are many types of swings that can be used by children with any kind of disability. Swings made from old tires and hung low to the ground may be easier for children with physical disabilities to use than other types of swings.

You might build a low slide that has a ramp leading to it. Make sure the ramp is long and only slightly inclined so that a child with limited motor ability can easily crawl or use a walker on it. The platform at the top of the slide should have railings and be big enough to park a walker and allow an adult to help a child down the slide. Make the slide extra wide so that two people can slide down together.

Mount old steering wheels at different heights in various places on the playground so that children with different disabilities can reach them. You might also make several play stations that will be fun for all children on the playground. One such station might be a music panel made of a number of things that make noises, or a panel of gadgets that a child can twist, turn, and pull. Or you might have a basketball station with low hoops at different heights so everyone can be successful.

The Daily Schedule

Making Environments Predictable

Most people are a little nervous when they enter a new situation but feel more comfortable as time goes by. Think back to your first visit to a new church, dentist, or community meeting. You may have felt a little nervous because you didn't know what would happen while you were there. You may not have known where to sit or hang your coat. You may have been wondering if you would like your new dentist or if you would have a cavity that needed filling. You were nervous because you couldn't predict what would happen.

Like you, all children need to know a little about what will happen during their time away from home. They need schedules and routines that are followed day after day—ways of doing things that are mostly the same. For children with cognitive disabilities or behavioral problems, having routines and sticking to them is especially important. For these children, changes can be quite upsetting.

Having schedules and routines does not mean that you do the same activity day after day. Instead, it means that your day has a predictable rhythm. Children quickly learn that after they wash their hands, they eat, then comes story and nap, and after that, outdoor play. They will eat different foods each day, read different books, and play with different things outside, but the order of activities will remain the same. Children also need to be given many opportunities to make choices and decisions about the children they want to play with and activities they want to do.

Schedules

Schedules outline the order in which you do certain activities every day. A daily schedule will help you organize your day around important activities and at the same time will make the environment more predictable for children. It will also make sure that you get around to important activities every day. Rather than setting rigid times for activities to begin and end, a schedule should describe the flow of the day's activities. A schedule should tell which activities follow each other and about how long children will spend doing those activities. *It is very important to remember that schedules should fit children, not the other way around.*

Instead of having set times for certain activities, it is helpful to think of your day as being divided into early morning, mid-morning, late morning, early afternoon, mid-afternoon, and late afternoon. Then you can decide on the types of activities that will take place during those periods. The activities and the amount of time you spend doing them will be a little different every day, but you will keep to the same order day after day.

The Active Learning Series offers a schedule for each different age group. A sample schedule for Ones is shown below. You can change this schedule to fit your children's needs.

Children arrive: Greeting

Routine care (breakfast, diapering, or going to the potty)

Self-directed activities in play areas

Midmorning: Snack

Planned play: teacher-directed activities for some

Outdoor time

Late morning: Lunch

Nap

Cleanup after lunch

Teacher-directed activities for toddlers who are awake

Early afternoon: Some napping toddlers get up

Routine care (snack, diapering, or going to the potty)

Planned play: teacher-directed activities for toddlers who are awake

Rest of napping toddlers get up

Mid-afternoon: Routine care

Teacher-directed activities for some, self-directed activities for others

Outdoor play time

Late afternoon: Self-directed activities in play areas

Routine care (diapering or going to the potty, clean-up, snack)

Talk to parents

Clean up room

Set up for next day

Schedules for infants. Each infant has his or her own clock for sleeping, eating, and playing, so each baby's schedule will be different. It's important to feed infants when they are hungry, allow them to sleep when they are sleepy, and play when they are playful, rather than trying to make them keep a schedule someone else has set. When babies' needs are met "on demand," they learn to trust others and feel secure.

Schedules for toddlers and preschoolers. When babies become toddlers, they are able to handle a little scheduling, although it is still important to stay in tune with each child's need to eat, sleep, or play. As you plan your schedule, you will want to plan time for the following activities:

- indoor and outdoor play
- free play, in which children choose most of their own activities
- directed play, in which children participate in a few activities led by adults
- independent play and small-group play
- quiet play and active play
- different kinds of activities such as art, music, and stories
- naps or rest
- snack or lunch
- toileting or diapering
- specific activities to promote certain skills

Planning the Daily Schedule for Children with Disabilities

Once you have set a schedule, you can use the Active Learning Series to decide which activities are best for a particular time period. The last portion of this manual will give you tips on adapting the Active Learning Series activities for children with disabilities.

You will not need to make major changes in your schedule for children with disabilities. However, children with disabilities often move more slowly than their peers, so you will need to plan carefully to be sure that children have enough time to move from one activity to the next. You will also need to plan time for children to receive therapy or extra physical care.

Transitions. For children with disabilities, you may need to allow a little more time during *transitions* between activities. Transitions, or changing from one activity to the next, need to be carefully planned for all children so that they go smoothly. Make sure you establish predictable routines for stopping one activity and beginning another, and stick to them. In addition to allowing a little more time for children with disabilities to make a transition, you may also need to ask some of the other children to help. For example, if ringing a bell signals cleanup time, you may want to ask a child who can hear to sign "cleanup time" to a child who is deaf. And be sure to give the children some warning before any activity change.

Planning time for therapy. Many children with disabilities receive some kind of therapy during the day. Sometimes a specialist may come into the child-care setting to work with the child. In this case you will need to schedule this visit with the therapist to make sure the child is not missing out on a favorite activity while he or she is in therapy. An even better solution is to plan so that the child can receive therapy while participating in the daily routines of the child-care setting.

When children are taken out of the room for therapy, they often have a hard time using the new skills that they have learned in other settings. For example, even if a child has been taught in therapy to pick up a spoon and put it into her mouth, she may not feed herself during lunch or snack. It would be better if the therapist were able to work with the child during lunch or snack, so that the child would be more likely to use the new skill. Work with therapists and other professionals to schedule their visits to make use of the activities going on in the child-care setting.

No matter who visits, you will be counted on to help the child practice his or her new skills whenever possible. For example, if a child is learning to pick up and then let go of an object, you might help the child practice this skill by encouraging him to drop blocks in a bucket, stones into water, or to bounce balls onto the floor. The caregiver and parent are the only people who can help a child practice these skills throughout the day, so your job is particularly important.

In some cases therapists will not visit the child-care setting at all. The child may get therapy in the home or at an office. In that case it's especially important for you to find out what is being taught, so that you can help the child practice while he is with you.

Routines

Regular routines, such as preparing for lunch or snack, diapering, or cleaning up can be used to help children feel secure and competent. This happens when adults help children learn exactly what to do and what to expect. For example, you might teach children that ringing a bell is the signal for the time to put away toys and wash hands for snack. When children follow this routine, they feel independent and good about themselves.

Different children might need to handle routines in different ways. For example, when saying goodbye to his parent, one child might need to sit in the teacher's lap for a few minutes as the parent goes out the door, while another might need her parent to play with her for five minutes before leaving. This is fine. What is important is that the child can count on certain things happening at the same time each day.

Use routine care as an opportunity to teach. You can help children learn during your daily routines. When you change a baby's diapers, be sure to talk to him or play a little game such as "This Little Piggy." When you help an older child take off her coat, count the buttons, sing a song, or ask her a question. In this way, you are making good use of every minute you have with a child.

Take your time during routine care. Don't try to take care of all of the children at one time. Take each child separately and play together as you do the tasks.

Adapting Routines to Meet the Needs of Children with Disabilities

Routines are especially important to children with disabilities. It often takes a lot of effort and practice for a child with a disability to learn a routine. A change in that routine can frustrate and upset the child. For some children with disabilities, routines become rituals, and the child feels like he *must* do one thing before he can do something else. It is very important to respect these needs. As with schedules, you will often need to allow more time for routines for children with disabilities.

■ *Greeting and Saying Goodbye*
It is important to start each day with a warm greeting to both the child and the parent. Some children with disabilities may greet you with a big smile and perhaps a hug, but others will not be as able to show their feelings. A child with cerebral palsy may have a hard time making her mouth form a smile; you will have to look for the twinkle in her eyes. Some children may look as though they don't care what happens, but they still need to feel loved and welcomed.

You will want to ask the parent of a child with disabilities if she or he has any special concerns that day. You may want to make a note of those concerns to be sure that you pass them on to your co-workers. Parents' concerns might relate to a child's hearing aids or other special equipment, or to new skills the child has learned that need practice during the day.

You may need to offer a child with a disability extra help to become involved in an activity. Some children easily move into activities alone or with others, but children with disabilities often have a hard time knowing what to do next. You might suggest an activity, lead the child to it, and help him or her get started. You might also help the child find a friend.

■ *Washing Hands*
Before eating and after toileting, all children must wash their hands. Children need to be able to reach the sink, so if your sink is too high, build a large wooden step stool that can be slipped under the sink.

All young children will need adult supervision when washing their hands. To prevent spread of disease, the steps outlined on page 46 must be followed when washing hands. If a group of children are washing their hands under the faucet, you may want to leave the water running until all of them are finished. Children

should dry their hands with their own towel, not a shared one. Paper towels are best because they can be thrown away after use.

For all children liquid soap is better than bar soap, which can grow germs. A liquid soap dispenser that is attached to the wall is easier to use than a bar of soap or a free-standing liquid dispenser, which can slip out of hands or be spilled.

■ Mealtime

Hold an infant in your arms while feeding him or her a bottle. This helps the baby feel loved and secure. Use a bib if the baby dribbles. Never prop a bottle, because propping a baby's bottle may lead to ear infections and doesn't give babies the cuddling they need.

Sit with the children at a small child-size table at meals and snacks. Children who use wheelchairs should be pushed up as close to the table as possible.

Allow the children to use small child-size pitchers to practice pouring into their cups. Expect some spills and be prepared for them with clean, damp sponges and have water nearby. You may want to use a small pitcher with a spout and lid to reduce spills. Cups with two handles, a spouted lid, and a weighted bottom are particularly easy for children with motor disabilities to use.

Mealtime is a good time to practice taking turns as children pass napkins or plates and bowls. Talk with the children as they eat, making sure each child gets a chance to speak. Some children with disabilities may have a difficult time getting into the conversation. Watch closely for clues that the child may have something to say, and help her find a chance to speak.

■ Tooth Brushing

Children should learn to brush their teeth after a meal. Each child should have a toothbrush labeled with his or her name. Toothbrushes should be stored standing up and should not touch each other. An upside-down egg carton with a slit for each toothbrush makes a good container. Keep the toothbrushes up high so that the children cannot play with other people's brushes.

All young children need help brushing their teeth. Children with disabilities may not have the motor ability to brush their teeth well by themselves, but give them as much independence as possible. Children with cleft palates and other mouth deformities may require special help when brushing their teeth. Ask for advice from parents or other specialists.

■ Nap and Rest

Babies and toddlers can easily sleep in cribs placed in a large room where other activities are going on. Be sure cribs are placed in quiet areas of the room where sleeping children can easily be seen by adults. For older children, the nap or rest space should be quiet and easily darkened.

Each child should be given a cot, mat, or crib that is not shared with anyone else. The cots, mats, or cribs should be at least two feet apart to prevent the spread of germs and should be arranged so that you can easily get to the children in an emergency.

Nap time often follows snack or lunch. Help children remove their shoes and place them in the same place every day, perhaps just under the cot or crib. If the child has a special blanket or stuffed animal, make sure it is within reach. You may want to sing a song or read a short story to calm the child once he or she is settled.

Children with disabilities may need some special care before a nap. You may need to remove a child's hearing aids or braces. You may need to position a child with cerebral palsy on a special mat. The child's parents or other specialists will give you information about preparing for nap time.

■ *Diapering and Toileting*

Change a child's diapers whenever they are wet or dirty; do not wait until a set time. Some older preschoolers with disabilities may wear diapers for a variety of reasons. These children need a private place where their diapers can be changed. Be sure to wash your hands and the child's hands each time after changing a diaper or helping a child in the bathroom.

All young children need toilets that are the right height. Potty chairs should not be used because they spread germs. If any child must use a potty chair, it must be dumped, washed, and disinfected after each use. Keep potty chairs in or near the bathroom and away from play spaces. Other children can use a standard toilet but may need a small stool to stand on and a child-sized seat that sits atop the regular toilet seat.

Children in wheelchairs who are toilet trained may need to be able to move from the wheelchair to the toilet easily. They will probably need help from you because it is hard for young children (who are often in a hurry) to take off their clothes and move quickly from the wheelchair to the toilet. However, remember that you are helping the child to become independent, so allow the child to do things for himself or herself as much as possible. Parents may need to be reminded to dress their children in clothing that is easy to manage.

Use the diapering or toileting time as a chance to talk to children. Give them the opportunity to learn independence by allowing them to button, zip, snap, and so forth.

■ *Personal Care*

A runny nose spreads infection. Wipe runny noses as often as necessary, using a fresh soft tissue for each child. Throw it away after using and wash your hands to prevent spread of germs. The child's hands should also be washed.

Children need their faces washed after eating. Get in the habit of using a separate damp napkin to give each child's mouth a quick swipe when needed. Many children can do this task themselves with a few reminders.

Wet clothes need to be changed immediately to prevent contamination of surfaces and to keep the child comfortable. Disinfect surfaces that have come in contact with wet clothing. Have parents send at least one change of clothes for each child, and be sure to have extras in the child care setting.

Help children stay clean. Roll up their sleeves and use bibs and smocks when they eat, paint, or do other messy activities. Children should wash their hands after playing outside. Make sure they get dirt out from under their fingernails, between their fingers, and on the backs of their hands.

Note: Some material in this section relies heavily on material found in *Integrated Child Care* by Sarah A. Mulligan, Kathleen Miller Green, Sandra L. Morris, Ted J. Maloney, Dana McMurray, and Tamara Kittelson-Alred, copyright 1992, by Communication Skill Builders, Inc., Tucson, AZ. Reprinted with permission.

Active Learning for Children with Disabilities

Adults, Children,
and Play

KEY POINTS

- Adults are the most important part of the child care environment.

- Children learn through playing.

- Because disabilities affect the way a child can play, they also affect what a child learns.

- Children learn from the adults and children who play with them.

The Importance of Play

Everyone thinks they know what play is, but you'll find that it is hard to describe. The same activity can be play to one person and work to another. Play depends on these things:

- the age of the person
- if the person can choose to do the activity
- if the activity is done just for pleasure

Children play naturally. Not only does play entertain and bring pleasure, but children also gain new skills and practice old ones when they play. It is likely that that young children learn more and better while they are playing than they do in teaching or training sessions. The Active Learning Series contains information about the importance of different kinds of play in the *Here's Why* page that comes before each section of activities. Reading it will help you understand how certain activities help children grow and develop.

Disabilities can limit children's play, so some children with disabilities may miss chances to learn. This is why caregivers need to be very aware of the developmental needs of children with disabilities and adapt play activities so that all children can participate.

Play Changes as Babies Grow

Play changes as babies become toddlers, as toddlers become preschoolers, and as preschoolers grow to become young children, adolescents, and adults. At first, babies play by watching and listening to the world around them. A bright mobile, a familiar face, fluttering leaves, birds singing, music playing—all interest a baby. Later, babies learn to use toys to make something happen. They may bang things to make noise or drop their spoons just to watch them fall. As babies grow older, they start using toys in the way they see others use real things. They will "cook" with a pot and pretend to eat with a spoon. Sometime later, they will begin using their eyes and hands together to make buildings with blocks, string beads, and put puzzles together. The Active Learning Series *Baby Can, Ones Can, Twos Can,* and *Threes Can* lists tell what typically developing children can do at various ages. The items on the lists also appear on each activity box to use as a guide for deciding if a particular activity is suitable for a given child.

Playing Equals Learning

Whenever children are playing, they are also learning—and having fun while they do it! When they drop blocks into a container, they are learning how to use their fingers—first to hold and then to let go. They also learn about the object they are using. They learn how heavy it is and whether it is rough or smooth, hard or soft. And when the block goes "plunk" as it hits the bottom of the container, they learn about the noise that blocks make when they are dropped. When children have learned all they can from this activity, they are no longer interested in dropping blocks into a container and start using blocks to stack and knock down or to make roads and cities.

When children play, they practice skills in all the developmental areas. As a toddler and a caregiver roll a ball to one another, the toddler is practicing motor skills as well as learning the social skill of taking turns. If the caregiver talks about the activity with the child— "Look at the ball! Here it comes! You got it! Now, roll it to me"—the child is also learning new words and ideas. Think about children who are working together to build a house out of old sheets and pieces of furniture. You will see the children talking to each other, to the adults in the room—even to themselves. They are practicing language skills. They are learning to cooperate and share as they work together to decide what their house should look like and how to move heavy furniture. They use their large muscles as they move chairs and tables to hold up the sheets. As they discover how to use tape, clothespins, and other things to hold the sheets in place, they are using cognitive (thinking) skills. Children are using their small muscles when they pinch the clothespins together and when they scribble a sign for over the door. Once the house is finished, playing "house" inside gives children a chance to practice self-help skills such as using a spoon or buttoning a coat.

As you can see, play is an important way for children to learn. That is why you set up your room with different kinds of play areas—to make sure children use many different kinds of skills as they play. The Active Learning Series suggests activities of different types to help children between the ages of infancy and four years learn.

Children with Disabilities and Play

Children with disabilities enjoy and need play, just as typically developing children do. Play is as important to the development of children with disabilities as it is to typically developing children. Yet because of a disability, some children may have trouble with certain kinds of activities. That makes your job as a caregiver even more important, because you will need to look for ways to help children participate in a wide variety of activities so that they develop their skills in all areas through play. You can do this by using the following ideas:

- Design spaces that allow children to be as independent as possible.
- Arrange schedules and routines in ways that help children make the most of their learning time.

- Interact with children in certain ways that help them play.
- Choose and adapt toys and activities so that children with disabilities can use them.

You have already learned a lot about making spaces and schedules work for children with disabilities. The next two major sections of the manual will cover the other two aspects of the learning environment: the ways adults talk and play with children and the toys, books, and other learning and playing materials in the room.

How Do Adults Help Children Play and Learn?

What is Learning?

Learning takes place in stages. Think about what it is like to teach a child to sing a song. First you teach the child the words and tune—you sing it over and over, and at times stop to let the child fill in the next word. After many days of singing the song, the child catches on and can sing it along with you, but not by herself. This stage is called *acquisition*—the child has all the skills needed to sing the song, but still needs a little help from you. The more you and the child sing, the more *fluent* the child becomes and the less help she needs from you. Soon, you'll find her singing the song to herself as she plays, whether or not you're around—that's called *maintaining* a skill. And you'll also discover that the child is singing the song on the way home on the bus or in the car or teaching it to other children or adults. *Generalization* is when a child can do a new skill in a different place from where he learned it.

Four Stages In Learning
- Acquisition—Learning to do the skill
- Fluency—Practicing the skill often enough that it comes naturally
- Maintenance—Doing the skill independently
- Generalization—Doing the skill in new places or at new times

Adults Help Children Learn by Joining in the Play

If you work in a center where several adults are in the room with you, take the opportunity every now and then to glance around the room and look at what the adults (not the children) are doing. If you do this often enough, you'll eventually notice that adults interact with children in different ways.

At some time, you might notice an adult putting on a real show—almost jumping up and down, dancing, or singing—to entertain a child. Other times you might notice an adult just sitting and watching the children play but not really interacting with the children. Adults also teach children—how to put paste on paper or play simple games, for example. Then there is the adult who just seems to like playing with the children. No matter what the children are doing, he's in there with them, playing and talking. This adult may get materials out for children to play with but lets each child decide how the materials are used. For example, the adult may get out a tub of rubber animals, watch to see how the children want to play with the animals, and then follow along.

All these roles—the entertainer, the teacher, the watcher, and the partner—are important. Every caregiver will be each of these at some time. But the partner role—joining in the play wholeheartedly—is the most important. Children learn best from adults who play *with* them. Children watch adults when they play and will often copy what they see. Playing with children also gives adults the chance to guide children's play in ways that will help them develop new skills or practice ones they have just learned.

Children who have disabilities may need help to get involved in play activities. Children who cannot get around on their own will need to be carried or led to play spaces. Sometimes, adults need to place children so that they can participate, perhaps positioning a child in a standing board or putting the child over a cushion to free his hands. Other children may not show much interest in doing in activities. Adults can help by offering them interesting toys, getting their attention, and showing them what to do with the toy. Children with visual impairments may need an adult to help them explore objects and surroundings with their other senses. Adults need to make it possible for a child with disabilities to become involved in play, either by setting up the environment or changing the activity to match what the child can do.

Guidelines for Playing with Children

1. *Have fun!* You don't always have to play with the children. In fact, children should have time to play together without an adult in the group, so enter into play activities that are fun for you.

2. *Read the child's cues.* Watch and listen to the child while you play. If the child seems to be getting bored, suggest another activity. Babies and young children don't stick to one activity for long, so be ready to move quickly to a new activity that interests the child. If the child is getting hungry or tired, stop the play for a snack or rest. Try to plan an activity that the child can master or finish based on age and ability.

3. *Let the child choose the activity and how to do it.* Then you can help the child learn even more. Use activities the child has chosen as a base for expanding and supporting learning. For example, if a child is working a simple four-piece puzzle of zoo animals and you want her to learn to put two words together, work with her on the puzzle and use phrases such as "funny monkey" or "big elephant."

4. Take turns. It's easier to teach a child what taking turns is all about if you start by taking turns with him in play activities. Of course a very young child might not want to take turns with you. That's fine. Just watch and talk about what he is doing.

5. Communicate with the child in many ways, especially by talking! Talk with the children as you play and give them many chances to talk. Make comments about what they are doing, ask questions, describe things around them. Although not all children will understand everything you are saying, even babies will be learning the sounds and rhythms of speech and storing up words to use later.

Don't talk too much and take over. Encourage the children to talk to each other and to you. And sometimes a child just wants some quiet time to think.

Talking is not the only way to communicate with children. Smiles, hugs, and just being interested are all important because they tell the child something. Use pictures, arrows, and sign language when you need to get across a point.

6. Challenge the child—just a little bit. Help the child to do something that's a little hard for him; make him stretch his mind. Encourage the child to work hard for goals you are pretty sure he can reach. Be sure the child can stop if the challenge is too much. He will always try again if he doesn't become frustrated.

7. Let the child discover "new" uses for toys. Don't insist that toys should be used in only one way. If children discover new uses for toys (for example, using Duplo™ blocks as people), go along with them. Anything is fine as long as no one or nothing gets hurt.

8. Let children play in their own style. Don't take over children's play. Set sensible limits, but let the children play in a way that is satisfying to them and follow along.

9. Help children get involved in play. Some children immediately start playing—alone or with others. Other children have a harder time getting involved in play. Go with a child like this to a space where another child is playing. Show her what she can do with the toys in the space and stay there to help her get started. Often, if you are playing with one child, other children will come and join in the play.

10. Help the child relate to other children. Babies, toddlers, and preschoolers often play near one another. You can help them tune into the play of other children by talking about what all the children are doing. You can help them get along better by helping them to respect the space and toys of others. And when they become interested in playing with each other, you can help them learn to work out any problems by talking things through.

Adults Help Children Learn by Planning and Setting Goals for Play

Typically developing children naturally learn through play what they are ready to learn, as long as the environment offers a variety of play choices. But this isn't always true for children with disabilities. Disabilities can prevent children from choosing some kinds of play, even if many opportunities are available. When children choose only a few kinds of play, they don't develop skills that other kinds of play teach. That is why it is important to have goals for play for children with disabilities—to make sure they develop skills in all areas.

Selecting goals for play can be a challenging task. Each child will have different needs and will enjoy doing different things. The important fact to remember is that you should select goals that will make a difference in a child's life. Target skills that help children "learn to learn" and become more independent.

Watch children carefully and make sure that they can take the next step when they are ready. For babies, this may mean that you put up a new picture where they can see it. For toddlers, you may introduce a word for a new food. For preschoolers, you may add new things to play with in the pretend play area. There are unlimited ways you can help children move ahead in their learning.

How do you know what goals to set for each child? By watching and listening to children, you can figure out what they can already do well, the new skills they are practicing, and what they can't do at all yet. Then you can set goals for a child to learn through play.

Tips for Setting Goals

- Watch the child carefully to see what he or she can do in each area of development. Check your ideas by asking parents about their child's skills.
- Use a developmental checklist like the *Baby Can, Ones Can, Twos Can, Threes Can* lists in the Active Learning Series to begin with. Use lists with other milestones if you wish.
- Set some goals that encourage the child to practice new skills, particularly in areas that aren't getting much attention. Find out what parents would like their child to learn next.
- Make sure there are lots of things the child can do that use skills he or she is practicing and that allow use of skills that are already well developed.
- Set a few goals for the next step the child might take. Then be sure that there are plenty of chances for the child to try each day.

- Be careful not to push the child to make too big a step. Set lots of tiny goals—not just big ones.
- Continue to observe the child. He or she might not be ready to work on *your* goals. The child might surprise you and really be working on something else.
- Change your goals to match the child's interests and path toward learning. Remember—your goals might not always be the right goals for that time.
- Change your goals as you see the child move on.

Children Are Learning All the Time

Children are always learning—but what they learn might not be what you expect. Setting goals makes it more likely that children get the experiences they need to move forward. But you must set these goals very carefully and place play materials in the child's environment that invite practice of a new skill. Be ready to make changes if things are not interesting to the child. When a child chooses a toy that is too difficult, perhaps a puzzle, for example, the child may lose interest and learn to think that puzzles are not fun and that he can't do them right. Of course, you do not want this to happen.

The most important thing you can do is to provide an environment that gives children many choices for interesting play. Then you can encourage children to work on the goals you set, and children can still have choices. For example, if a child needs play experiences in using large muscles, you can help her choose from among several activities such as crawling after you on foam mats, rolling a ball toward a friend, or swinging. Children will learn the most when they can be interested all the time, experiment and explore, do things for themselves, use their imaginations, and listen and talk with others.

You can work on several goals at the same time when you are playing with a child or when you are providing routine care. For example, while gently pushing a baby in a swing, stand in front of the child and make noises that you have heard the baby make. This way, you are helping the child develop balancing skills and language skills at the same time. *Whatever you are doing, give children reasons to talk.* Show the child something interesting and ask questions about it. Give the child choices and ask the child to tell you what toy he wants or what kind of juice he would like.

Be sure that your goals encourage and do not limit learning. Avoid making children wait with nothing to do, listen when they are not interested, or do things that are too hard. Tune into the children and allow learning to take off!

Helping Children
Relate to Others

KEY POINTS

- Social skills are important for the total development of a person.

- Social skills emerge at different ages.

- Children with disabilities may need adult help to develop social skills.

- Adults can do certain things to help children develop social skills and appropriate behaviors.

Social skills are the behaviors that people need in order to get along with others and to build satisfying relationships. Before the age of two, most of a child's important social experiences are with parents or caregivers. With the exposure to group settings, many children are interacting with peers at even earlier ages. Adults are still very important in a child's life for many years, but between the ages of two and three, other children also become important in the social lives of young children. Peers become more important as the child grows older.

Older children who have good social skills are liked by their playmates and adults. You will see such children leading other children in play, sharing, showing affection, helping others, and responding to the play interests of other children. They usually feel good about themselves and are interested in learning about the world around them.

Children and adults who have good social skills get along better in life. They tend to be more successful in school and at work. They have important and long-lasting relationships with other people. Many children who are cared for at home learn social skills by being part of a family, but as more children are cared for outside the home, it is important for caregivers to know how to nurture social development in child-care settings. Caregivers who know about social development will work to help each child develop:

- a positive opinion of himself or herself
- trust and respect for others
- specific behaviors that help the child get along with others

It takes a long time for children to learn social skills. Infants, one-year-olds, and two-year-olds will be unable to take turns and share. Older preschoolers will just be learning to get along with one another. It's important to have realistic expectations for what young children can handle in a group.

How Do Social Skills Develop?

The most important building block of good social skills is a secure attachment between an infant and the significant adults—the parent and caregiver. When you lovingly hold and feed a baby, when you respond to a baby's cry, when you give a baby your time and attention, you help the baby feel loved and secure. The relationship between you and the child that develops from your care and attention gives the baby the security needed to relate to other children and adults. The Active Learning Series contains suggestions for relating to children of each age group under the heading *Helping Babies* [or *Ones, Twos,* or *Threes*] *Feel Special.* These guidelines should be kept in mind throughout the day and during all activities.

Like other skills, social skills develop gradually over time. Babies are born with early social skills, such as gazing at a human face and smiling. Babies will just smile or gaze on their own without having to be taught. But it takes two people for social skills to become a real part of a baby's behavior. When a baby smiles, someone needs to be there to smile back—to reward or *reinforce* the behavior. The more a skill is reinforced, the stronger it becomes. A baby's mother, father, and caregivers are the most important reinforcers of the infant's social skills. This reinforcement happens naturally. Without even thinking about it, adults reinforce a baby's social skills during play together simply by showing their enjoyment.

Babies and children also learn social skills by watching and imitating other children and adults. Whether or not parents realize it, they have been teaching their baby to coo from the day he was born by holding him, gazing into his eyes, and making comforting noises. The baby hears these noises and soon tries making noises on his own. As the parents and child make noises back and forth, the child is learning to take turns.

It will be a long time before the baby can successfully take turns. But this is the beginning of years of learning. As the baby learns one skill, parents and caregivers help the baby develop more skills by taking play one step further. Parents will first echo their baby's cooing sounds, and then parents will introduce a new cooing sound. Soon, the baby will learn to make a similar sound. Adults and babies love playing these games together. It's fun for parents and caregivers to see babies gaining new skills, so parents get reinforced, too!

Remember that children do not copy only the good things that adults and older children do. They can learn troublesome behaviors by watching others, too. A toddler who hears yelling or sees others treated unkindly will quickly learn these unwanted behaviors. That's one reason why it is so important to treat children kindly and gently. Then they learn to be kind and gentle, too.

Later, other children also become important teachers of social skills. When watching or playing with others, toddlers learn who they are and what others expect of them. Just like adults, young children reinforce the social behaviors of their playmates. They learn to take turns, cooperate, share, and respect the needs of others.

Goals for Social Development

Young children need to develop skills that will help them play happily with other children. Here are several tips for helping children develop socially. Although there are many other social skills for children to learn, the ones listed below will help children be good playmates.

Tips for Infants, Toddlers, and Two-Year-Olds

- Help children learn to be gentle with others. Teach this by being gentle yourself.
- Help infants, one-year-olds, and two-year-olds not to take toys that others are using but to get one for themselves.
- Encourage children to help out and to show affection and sympathy.

Tips for Children Two or Older

- Show children how to respond when other children invite them to play.
- Help children learn to share toys and take turns, but never force this. Be sure there are plenty of things that do not need to be shared.
- Help children pay attention to what other children are doing.
- Encourage children to imitate the positive play of other children.
- Help children organize play activities with other children.
- Help children learn to make decisions.

In most cases, you do not need to plan special activities just for social skills development—you can simply help children learn and use new social skills as they do activities and play throughout the day.

Effects of Disabilities on Social Development

How Disabilities Can Delay Social Skills Development

Children learn social skills when what they do is *reinforced,* or followed by a pleasant event such as a hug, smile, or extra attention. They also learn by *watching* and *imitating* others. But the presence of a disability can delay the natural learning of social skills.

- *Disabilities can prevent the reinforcement of a social behavior.* Smiling is an important social behavior that must be reinforced to last. A baby who is visually impaired will smile as a reflex in early infancy but may not continue to smile as he grows older because he cannot see an adult return his smile. Likewise, a baby who coos but cannot hear her mother coo in return may not continue to coo. Also, she will be less likely to try new sounds because she has not heard her mother make new cooing sounds.

■ *Children with some types of disabilities develop social skills differently from typically developing children.* Sometimes, the child may simply be slower at learning new social skills. It may take a long time to learn about taking turns, to grasp the rules of a game, or to understand how to get someone to play. It may be especially hard or impossible for children with some disabilities to look other people in the eye or to smile. Some children have unusual behaviors or mannerisms that affect how comfortable others are when they are around them, and some may not like to be touched.

■ *Disabilities may keep children from showing their interest or delight in ways that adults and other children can easily understand.* A child with visual impairments may not make eye contact to let a playmate know she's listening. Children struggling to control their muscles may have a hard time getting out a giggle or a smile at the right moment. When this happens, adults and children can sometimes get tired or frustrated and stop playing with the child because the child doesn't seem to respond. Then the child's social behaviors are not reinforced, so they decrease. An adult must be patient and keep trying to help such children develop socially and must encourage typically developing children to keep trying, too.

■ *Disabilities affect the social skills a child learns through watching and imitating the people around him or her.* Some children with disabilities may have trouble picking up on the social signals of other children. Such children may not know when someone is interested in playing or how a playmate might be reacting. It will take such children longer to figure out the unspoken rules of play or what is expected of them as a playmate. It may be just as difficult for the child with disabilities to send social signals as it is to receive them. For example, he may have trouble letting the friend know he wants to move on to a new activity or that he does not like what the friend is doing.

■ *Specific types of disabilities present their own challenges.* Children with physical disabilities may not have the muscle control needed to play with other children, children with hearing loss may not hear requests from other children to play, and children with visual impairments may not be able to see the look on a playmate's face that shows what she is thinking or how she is feeling.

Using the Active Learning Series to Help Children Develop Social Skills

Children learn social skills as they play, just as they do other kinds of skills. All the activities in the Active Learning Series encourage learning of social skills while the child is working on another skill. Talking with the children as you do the activities together is one very important way in which children learn social skills. If you watch and listen carefully, you will see that children will imitate the words you use and the way you act.

Begin helping children develop social skills by planning. The table below gives you some information about the social development of children at certain ages. (It is important to remember that, just as with the *Can* lists in the Active Learning Series, the lists are only general guidelines. They cannot be used to find out if a child is developing normally.) Following each social skill are numbers of activities in the Active Learning Series that may help nurture the development of the skill. Use the table to help you identify goals and activities for social development for children at certain ages.

Age in months	Social Skill	Activity Numbers
		Infants
0–3	■ likes to look at a human face	4, 9, 31, 253, 278
	■ coos to keep an adult's attention	19, 20, 23, 25
	■ cries when uncomfortable or bored	22
	■ gazes into the eyes of an adult	176, 181
	■ smiles when happy; scowls when unhappy	24, 27, 244
2–6	■ responds differently to people she knows	9
	■ gets an adult's attention by kicking legs, waving arms, cooing, gazing, or crying	25, 27, 34
	■ coos back and forth with an adult (turntaking)	4, 9, 31, 198, 213
	■ plays simple games	23, 38, 67, 71, 72, 159, 172, 199, 204, 214, 216

		Infants (cont.)
6-12	■ follows or clings to a loved adult	35, 76, 295
	■ pays attention to names	29, 47, 210, 280
	■ copies simple actions	38, 169, 174, 189, 214, 219, 309
	■ recognizes self in mirror or picture	160, 218, 278, 289, 306

		Ones
12–24	■ calls self by name	10, 25, 28, 32, 42, 58, 66, 233, 328, 338
	■ involves self in play	all activities
	■ helps put things away	24, 33, 43, 44, 72, 260
	■ copies others' actions	19, 30, 35, 37, 47, 48, 56, 60, 117, 187, 193, 205–231, 308

		Twos
24–36	■ talks to make contact with adult	36, 44, 204, 292, 294
	■ begins play with other children by getting near, touching, giving toys, receiving toys, looking	33, 35, 50, 57, 62, 91, 174, 286, 330, 362
	■ begins to play house and pretend	225–254, 269
	■ takes part in simple group activities	2, 24, 63, 101, 108, 119, 150, 163, 268, 276
	■ plays next to another child but doesn't usually cooperate	30, 197, 258, 264

		Threes
36–48	■ likes to play with other children	29, 38, 48, 52, 85, 98, 100, 219
	■ occasionally shares toys	74, 313, 316, 370, 375, 399
	■ takes turns with help from adults	57, 89, 125, 166, 192, 276, 313, 316, 402, 420, 434
	■ pretends	47, 66, 77, 123, 199, 200, 204, 221–250, 257, 258
	■ often cooperates with other children	3, 4, 61, 62, 73, 121, 191, 193, 422

Encouraging Children to Include Others

Children with disabilities need help from adults to develop socially. Everybody benefits when children with and without disabilities play together, but they may not play together initially without adult help. Children with disabilities may not be chosen as playmates by typically developing children unless an adult encourages them to play together. It often takes children with disabilities longer to get to the play area, longer to say something, and longer to be understood. Young children are not aware of these problems and keep on with their play. Too often the child with disabilities gets left behind or overlooked. Although independence is an important goal, without an adult's help, children with disabilities may not have the chance to socialize. As a caregiver, you can help children of various abilities to play together.

Tips for Helping Children to Include Others

- Show love and acceptance toward children with disabilities. *It's fun to paint with Brooke. It makes her so happy to have you beside her.*
- Include the child as an equal in all activities.
- Read books in the classroom that show children with disabilities in a positive light.
- Decorate your room with pictures of children with disabilities doing everyday activities with other children.
- Have a child with disabilities sit next to a very well liked, typically developing child.
- Show children that you are pleased when they choose a child with disabilities as a playmate. *I'm glad you're playing with Jerome. You'll have fun together.*
- Play along with the children and make sure each child has the opportunity to talk and play.

Strategies for Helping Children Develop Social Skills

Keep groups small. Only older preschoolers are ready to play in groups. When you plan groups, keep them small—only two or three children. An adult should always be present to ease difficult interactions such as grabbing toys. Children should be free to leave groups as they lose interest.

Have the right number of materials in group play. Infants and one- and two-year-old children can't be expected to share, so supply enough materials for everyone. Older two-year-old and some three-year-old children might be able to share for a short time if they know that they will quickly regain the item.

Give similar toys to two children and encourage them to play beside each other. Even though the two children are not playing with each other, they arc learning about how to play together. When they are older, they will be better able to cooperate, share, and take turns if they have had earlier opportunities just to sit beside another child and play with a similar toy.

Model the behaviors you want children to learn. The first place to start in helping children learn social skills is to do what you want them to do, or *model* the behavior. The child will watch you and copy what you are doing. Make a point to use behaviors that you want the child to develop, such as smiling, taking turns, and asking without grabbing. Children with disabilities often don't know how to get other children to play. They often do not know how to act when other children show an interest in playing with them, so these are also behaviors you will want to model.

Prompt desired behaviors. *Prompting* means telling or showing a child what to do. There are many times when you will want to prompt children to behave in a certain way.

Simply telling a child what you expect can be a prompt. You may prompt children to show them how to get other children to play with them.

Here is some play dough. Show it to Rosemarie and ask if she wants to play.

Shawn is all alone in the block area. Let's go together and see if he wants to play.

You may also want to prompt children to respond to other children.

Robin asked you if you wanted to wear the long gloves. Say yes.

Emily is giving you the crayons. Take them.

Brent is looking at you. I think he wants to play with the bulldozer, too. Show him how it works. Then he can use one, too.

Prompts are a good way to teach children to help others or to show sympathy or affection.

Shanessa's truck went behind the door. Do you want to help her get it?

Adam is feeling sad. Let's give him a hug to make him feel better.

Kathryn is happy to see you again. Wave back at her.

Prompts are useful in teaching older children to share or to take turns.

Kenric wants a turn on the swing. Tell him that he can have a turn after you have three more pushes.

Maya, it's time for Dawn to have a turn at the water table. Come over here and let's dig in the sand together.

Naomi, please let Brian have some of the peanut butter now for his cracker.

You may use prompts to help children imitate behaviors. Not all prompts are things you say; sometimes you might guide a child through a behavior—that's a prompt, too.

Do you see how Phillip is helping Carrie put the blocks in the bucket? Let's go help. The caregiver puts a block in the child's hand, leads her to the bucket and helps her drop it in. *You dropped it in!*

See Jerry? He's painting. You paint, too. The caregiver puts a paintbrush in the child's hands and places the paper where she can easily reach it.

Help children notice what is going on around them by pointing it out and commenting on it. Many children with disabilities are not aware of the things going on around them. Tell children what is happening.

I am fixing your juice now.

Jennifer is making a tall tower of blocks.

Chris and Twanna are washing the baby dolls.

You will need to show children with hearing loss what is going on in the room. If you can, use sign language or gestures to communicate with the child.

Move children through the motions. Sometimes children with disabilities are not able to participate fully in an activity because of their disability. When this is the case, help the child participate by moving him or her through the motions. For example, if a group of children are doing a fingerplay along with the caregiver, you may need to take the child's hands and help him do the fingerplay.

Practice some skills ahead of time. It may be harder for some children to learn skills that are difficult for all young children to learn, such as taking turns and sharing. You may want to work with these children by yourself before you expect them to cooperate with other children. Let the children practice the skills with you many times before you expect them to use the skills with their playmates.

How to Help Children Act in Acceptable Ways

Have reasonable expectations. Expect children to behave age-appropriately. Do not expect a one-year-old to know how to take turns or to share. Expect young children to be fussy or irritable when they are tired. The Active Learning Series can help you determine the expectations that are appropriate for children of certain ages. Read the following sections: *Handling Problems; Helping Babies* [or *Ones, Twos,* or *Threes*] *Feel Special;* and the *Can* lists.

Be consistent. Children need to know what to expect. Stick to established rules and routines. Let children know that certain behaviors are valued (such as showing affection or helping to clean up) and that others are not valued (such as hitting or grabbing). Gently let the child know that you approve or disapprove. Let a child know that hurting someone else is never allowed.

Set clear expectations for behavior. Let children know their limits. Set simple rules, and gently and consistently enforce them. Tell children what they are supposed to do. Instead of saying, "Stop hitting," you might take the child's hands, look her in the face, and say, "Use words." Instead of telling a child not to stand on the table, say, "Stand on the floor," as you gently place her on the floor.

Let behaviors have logical consequences. Children learn more easily when consequences are naturally connected to behaviors. If a child throws sand, removing him from the sandbox would be better than making him lose a turn on the swing. If a child pulls all the toys off a shelf, having him help you put them back is better than making him sit in a chair by himself for a minute.

Reward appropriate social behaviors. When children behave appropriately, notice what they have done. There are many ways to do this. Sometimes, just saying "Thank you" or "That's a good idea" will do. Other times, a hug or smile lets children know that they've done something you like.

Adapting Activities and Materials for Children with Disabilities

The Active Learning Series contains activities designed to help young children learn. These activities can be used with all children, with or without disabilities, if you are willing to change some of the materials you use and perhaps the way you do the activity. Depending on the type of disability a child has and the degree of involvement, your changes may range from none at all to some complicated changes in toys or equipment. For example, some children with health impairments can participate in most activities without changing them in any way. However, on some occasions, the child may be too weak or tired to participate at all. Children with hearing loss require adaptations in activities that depend on communication. Children with visual disabilities need more adaptations in materials and activities than do perhaps any other group of children with disabilities.

Planning Activities to Help Children Learn

Encouraging Children to Learn by Doing

Planning is particularly important when you are working with children with disabilities. You must plan to make sure their play helps them learn in all developmental areas. For example, children who are blind typically do not move around in spaces the way sighted children do, so it is important to plan activities that encourage children with limited vision to move around and use their big muscles. You might notice that some children, whether or not they have a disability, like to do the same type of activity most of the day. Planning an interesting new activity will help get them involved in other types of play so that they will practice new skills.

The way you set up the children's environment can encourage children to choose activities that foster development in a specific area. For example, in the block corner, plan for several activities that nurture a child's fine motor development. Activities might include stacking blocks to match the height of other objects in the room or dropping blocks into holes cut in boxes. As children move among centers in the room, they choose activities within those centers planned by caregivers to help certain skills develop.

During each week, you will want to plan for quiet and active and for indoor and outdoor activities. You will want to set up the room so that children can be alone, with a friend, or in a group. Include activities for art, music, and drama. It's a good idea to repeat some activities that children enjoy because this helps them learn ideas and words. Children also enjoy repeating activities. You can see this when they ask for a favorite story over and over again.

Writing an Activity Plan

To help children learn, you need to plan what activities you are going to add to the toys and materials that are already in the room. Remember that very young children have short attention spans and like to change toys and activities often. This is also true for some children with disabilities, especially those with cognitive disabilities or behavioral problems. The Active Learning Series has many suggestions for activities that children with and without disabilities can enjoy doing together. The important thing to remember is that some of the activities will have to be adapted for children with disabilities—more about this later.

When you begin planning for children, you need to think of teacher-directed activities to add to the play children choose to do on their own. The daily plan can help you think of new toys to bring out that day and ways to change activity centers. Each of the Active Learning Series books contains directions for writing a daily activity plan as well as a form to use. On this form you may write down the names of the activities you will do with each child during the week. When planning for children with disabilities, you may want to add a row to each day's plan and list special goals that have been set by the child's parents or specialists, and activities that can help the child reach those goals. In addition to the activities in the Active Learning Series, you may want to write some activities of your own to follow up on the suggestions given by the child's parents or therapists.

Planning for Children with Disabilities

Like typically developing children, children with disabilities have their own patterns of what they can and cannot do. Children with disabilities will often have uneven development. A three-year-old child who is in a wheelchair may have most of the same skills other three-year-olds have but may not be able to do some of the physical skills that a one-year-old can do. You will want to plan to do some physical activities with this child, but choose activities that are on the child's *developmental level.* Educators talk about the developmental level of children to describe what skills a child has. The educator may say that a child's overall developmental level is like that of a two-year-old. This means that the child's skills are like those of a typically developing two-year-old, no matter what the actual age of the child is. A child's developmental level does not tell you how smart the child is or how much the child can learn. It simply describes what the child can do at a specific time.

Children with disabilities may be at one developmental level in one area and at another developmental level in another area. An educator may say that a child's motor developmental level is four years (meaning that he has motor skills like most four-year-old children) but that he has a communication developmental level of two years (meaning that he uses words like a typically developing two-year-old does).

How to Find the Right Activities for Each Child

- *Start with the* Baby, Ones, Twos, *or* Threes Can *Lists.*
  The Active Learning Series contains lists of skills— *Baby, Ones, Twos,* or *Threes Can* Lists—that describe what typically developing children can usually do at certain ages. You can use the *Can* lists to choose activities for children with disabilities, but because of the uneven development of children with disabilities, you might need to use several lists for each child.

- *Begin by looking at the* Can *list for the age the child is.*
  If a child with disabilities is three years old, start with the list in *Active Learning for Threes.*

- *Watch and think about the child.*
  Using the *Can* list, put the child's initials beside the items on the list that he or she can do or is beginning to be able to do. When you are finished, go back and look at the initialed items. In what

developmental area are the skills the child uses when doing that item—cognitive, fine motor, gross motor, communication, adaptive, and/or social or emotional?

- *Look for each child's pattern of strengths and needs according to developmental area.*
  You might find that a three-year-old child with hearing loss can do all of the motor and adaptive skills and many of the cognitive skills on the *Threes Can* List ("puts together two halves to make a whole," "does an easy five-to-ten piece puzzle," "walks heel to toe"), but few of the language skills ("names two or three colors or shapes").

- *When you notice that the child is unable to do things on the list, drop back a year to the previous age group's* Can *list.* Look for items that offer a chance to practice skills in the weak developmental area. Ask yourself, "Can the child do this skill?" You may find that the child with hearing loss can do some of the items on the *Twos Can* list that have to do with language ("listens to a five-minute story with pictures," or "identifies six body parts in a picture when asked"). The child may be using sign language to respond to your words, expressions, and gestures. With this child, you will choose activities from the *Threes* manual for all developmental areas except communication. You would use the *Twos* manual to choose communication activities and adapt them according to the needs of the child.

When choosing activities for children with disabilities, it is important to follow two guidelines.

1. Use activities that are age-appropriate. Whenever possible, choose activities that children the same age are doing. Sometimes children with disabilities cannot do the same things and do not have the same skills as other children their age, and you will have to choose an activity planned with younger children in mind. This can be a problem for older children doing the activity. They might not be attracted to the activity because the materials are not interesting to them. In addition, it is not age-appropriate behavior for older children to play with toys that have been designed for much younger children. When this is the case, adapt the activity and the materials so that the child can practice the needed skills in an appropriate way. For example, if a three-year-old child with mental retardation enjoys making sounds with a baby rattle, substitute age-appropriate toys that make sounds when they are shaken, such as tambourines or maracas.

Whatever their level of development, children should use toys that are meant for their age. When older children play with toys for much younger children, other children think they are like babies and do not want to play with them. This is especially true the older a child gets. Infants—both with and without disabilities—should use toys made for infants. Likewise, three-year-olds, regardless of their level of development, should play with toys made for three-year-olds. If an older child shows great interest in toys made for younger children, try to substitute an age-appropriate toy with a similar function.

Children with disabilities may miss learning important skills needed for further learning unless a parent or caregiver helps the child practice them in play. Sometimes you will really be challenged to help the child learn a skill in an age-appropriate way. For example, you would not want to teach a two-year-old child with hearing loss to babble a string of sounds because that's not age-appropriate. But the child needs to be able to make individual sounds to be able to move on in speech development, so you will want to find an age-appropriate way to help the child develop that skill. While you would not expect a child who has little speech to sing a song, you can still use an age-appropriate activity as an opportunity to help the child learn to make speech sounds. You might sing songs such as "Baa-baa Black Sheep," "The Wheels on the Bus," and "Old McDonald Had a Farm" and pause to let the child (with your help) make the noises. This shows you how the child can practice needed skills while doing an age-appropriate activity.

2. Choose activities with their functional value in mind. Children should not be taught to do a certain task just because it appears on a skill list. The task should have some real value. The task should lead to other, more difficult skills, or it should have some practical value by itself. For example, two-year-old children enjoy putting large pegs in a pegboard. This activity helps them develop fine motor control while they are also having fun. A four-year-old with cerebral palsy may have a difficult time putting pegs in a pegboard and may not like using the large pegs used by younger children. The functional value of this activity is to develop control of the small muscles. You might decide that a better activity to develop small muscle control for this child would be learning to zip his coat. Being able to zip his coat like other four-year-olds will help the child develop the needed skill while at the same time allowing the child to become more independent. The increased self-esteem the child will feel because he is able to put on and zip his coat like his friends has far more value than putting pegs in a pegboard.

Adapting the Active Learning Series for Children with Disabilities

The sections that follow are about adapting Active Learning Series activities for children with different types of disabilities. Adaptations for each disability are discussed separately.

You will notice that sections do not appear for children with health impairments, behavior problems, or speech and communication disabilities. You probably will not need to change the activities in the series for children with these disabilities, but you will need to keep each child's needs in mind. Ask the doctor or parents of a child with health impairments to advise you about caring for the child. Show them a list of typical activities and ask if they have any concerns about the child's participation in any of the activities.

The goal for children with behavior problems is to encourage them to interact positively with peers and adults. Tips for helping children are contained in the *Helping Children Relate to One Another* section in this book and in the Active Learning Series in the *Handling Problems* section. In most cases, implementing these suggestions consistently will be sufficient. If there is a particular problem, the advice of a specialist may be needed.

Children who understand language but who cannot clearly say the words have speech problems. The tips for adapting activities for listening and talking for children with physical disabilities may also be useful for children with speech problems. Children who have difficulty understanding what others say or who cannot express themselves have communication disabilities. They may also have trouble making speech sounds. For helpful tips, read the information on listening and talking with children with cognitive disabilities.

Activity Boxes for Children with Disabilities

The Active Learning Series includes many ideas for activity boxes. When you put everything you need for one kind of activity into a box or dishpan, you have made an activity box. This helps you keep many different things ready for children to play with without taking up much room. Activity boxes help you get set up quickly because you won't have to run around at the last minute to find the toys you need. You can keep activity boxes in a closet or on a shelf. Label each box so that you know what's inside. A picture or a real toy glued on the box will tell the children what's inside. Be sure that your boxes also contain toys that have been adapted for children with disabilities. You will think of other boxes, too, especially as children with disabilities are included in your child-care setting.

Before you put things back into an activity box, remember to clean what needs cleaning. If you are careful to do that, you can be certain that anything you take out of an activity box will be clean the next time you need it.

Active Learning for Children with Cognitive Disabilities

At age three, Evie, who has a cognitive disability, enjoys coming to day care. She has been coming since she was six months old, so we've had a chance to watch her grow up.

When she was a baby, she didn't learn things as quickly as the other children we cared for, but she did learn. Every day, we did activities with her from the Active Learning for Infants. *Even after her first birthday, we used the activities for infants much of the time, but used activities in the* Active Learning for Ones *as often as we could. When we played "Follow the Leader," one of us carried Evie with us and helped her do just what the leader did. When we played "Step Over the Line," the other children stepped over a piece of masking tape taped to the floor. Evie could do it, too, if we held her hands.*

As Evie and the other children got older, including Evie in the activities for children her age meant allowing her to do the activity in her own way. For example, one day when Evie was three, we did the Smell-Taste Surprises activity from the Active Learning for Threes *book. We put tuna fish, orange slices, and peanut butter in separate containers with lids. Then we asked the children to close their eyes, smell, and guess what was in the container. Evie watched the other children. When it was her turn, she looked in the container first, closed her eyes, and then smelled. She didn't know the name of tuna fish or oranges, but she did know peanut butter and proudly said it out loud. After the activity was over, we let Evie and the other children smell the foods again and gave each child a little to taste. We made sure we told Evie the name of each food again.*

*T*ypically developing children learn many skills simply by watching others, but children with cognitive disabilities may need your help to learn to perform many tasks. Like all babies, infants with cognitive disabilities need caregivers who make sure that they have interesting things to look at, hear, touch, smell, and taste. Even if a child with a cognitive disability does not show much interest in the world around him, keep offering a variety of experiences. Point out things in the environment and talk about them, even though the child may not understand right now. Progress may be slow, but each experience a child has is important to his development. The Active Learning Series will give you many ideas for activities you can do with children with cognitive disabilities that will be fun and help them learn new skills, too. You won't need to do many things differently to make the activities appropriate for infants and children with cognitive disabilities.

As a child with cognitive disabilities gets older and begins to develop more complex skills, some special approaches will be helpful. These approaches will be useful for teaching all young children, so don't limit their use just to children with cognitive disabilities.

- *Change a baby's position often so that she will experience new sensations.* When the baby is lying down and awake, try placing her in different positions, lying on one side and then the other, so that she can see the room around her from different perspectives. At other times, have the child sit in an infant seat, propping her head if necessary. Carrying a baby in a frontpack or backpack, making sure the baby's head is firmly supported, also allows a baby to experience new things.

- *Use words the children can understand in simple, short sentences.* Talking is most effective when you make eye contact with the baby and talk about what is going on at the time.

- *Vary active and quiet activities.* Children with cognitive disabilities may have short attention spans, so plan brief activities and switch between active ones and quiet ones. Plan for rests during the day. Children have difficulty going from a busy activity to rest, so plan a "wind-down" activity just before rest time.

- *Break down a skill or activity into small steps.* Don't expect a child to do all of the activity or practice the whole skill until he is ready. Until then, let the child do just a part. For example, a child who cannot put all the rings on the stack toy should be allowed to stack one, two, or three and feel successful.

- *Skills can be broken down into parts and each part learned one at a time.* Show the child how to do each part and then help her become good at it. For example, unzipping a coat can be divided into two parts: (1) grasping the zipper pull, and (2) pulling the zipper pull down. You might begin by helping the child grasp the zipper pull. Fasten a small object to the pull to make it easier to grasp. Holding your hand over his, help him zip. As the child becomes better at zipping, let go of his hand when you are close to the end of the zipper, letting him finish the job by himself. Gradually encourage the child to zip more of the zipper by himself until he is able to do all of it.

- *Guide a child with cognitive disabilities through the action.* Whenever you do an activity, it is helpful to show a child what to do and then guide her through the motions. For example, if you are doing a fingerplay, hold the child's hands in yours and help her do the motions. When the child begins making some of the motions on her own, praise her no matter how well she does them, and let her do them by herself. When you give directions, stay close to a child with cognitive disabilities until you are sure he knows what to do.

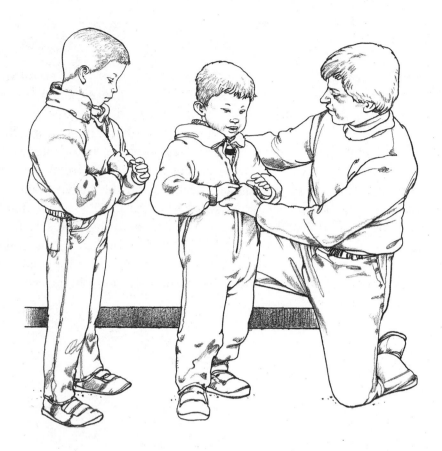

■ *Practice, practice, practice.* Children with cognitive disabilities may need many more opportunities to practice a skill before they learn it. When planning when you will do activities, allow time for the child who wants another turn. Plan to repeat activities more often if the child is interested.

■ *Praise success.* Independence is a major goal for all children. Praise children for trying to do something without adult help, no matter how well or how poorly it is done. Help a child achieve success. For example, if a child cannot put wooden pieces in a simple puzzle, guide the child's hands to the right place. Then praise him for fitting in the pieces.

Active Learning for Children with Cognitive Disabilities

The major goal in adapting toys for children with cognitive disabilities is to give developmentally appropriate experiences using age-appropriate toys. You can generally find an age-appropriate substitute for a toy that a child seems to like. For example, if a three-year-old child with cognitive disabilities shows a lot of interest in a baby's cribside activity board, you might prepare a box of items that do the same sorts of things that the items on the activity board do. You might include an egg timer with a dial that turns, springs that can easily be pushed together to bounce (make sure they are safe for the child), a squeeze horn, and a flashlight. It's still okay for the child to play with the baby's activity board once in a while, as long as he has other age-appropriate toys that interest him and help him develop the skills he needs.

Books and pictures. Until you begin doing group activities for listening and talking (at about age two), you won't need to adapt Active Learning Series activities for children with cognitive disabilities. Once you begin group activities, it may be wise to seat children with cognitive disabilities next to you when you read a story to a group. Make sure other children in the group also get this privilege on occasion. This way, you can let the child turn the pages when you are ready, thus keeping his attention. Allow children to listen to stories in any posture—lying down, sitting, standing, or leaning. Don't get upset if a child wanders away from the story group. Gently guide him back if you feel that he can still pay attention.

Short stories and rhymes are usually better choices than long stories for children with cognitive disabilities, as is true for most young children. Giving a child his own book to hold while you read may help keep his attention.

Conversation. Talk to a child with cognitive disabilities using short, simple sentences and words he can understand. Use gestures. Even if a child doesn't talk, he's learning when you talk to him. When possible, use real things to show children with cognitive disabilities what you are talking about.

Adapting Activities for Physical Development

*T*he muscle control of children with cognitive disabilities may be behind that of their peers, and you may need to find equipment that is easier to manage. Toys and materials that you might use with children with physical disabilities might also be useful with children with cognitive disabilities who lack good coordination. For example, beanbags are easier to catch than balls, and it is easier to push a riding toy than it is to pedal. When playing catch with a ball, you may sit on the floor across from a child and roll the ball into the V created by his outstretched and open legs.

Free play can be so exciting for some children that they cannot become involved in an activity. In this case, you may help the child by planning ahead of time what the child might do, leading him to that activity and staying with him to get him started.

Children with cognitive disabilities, like most children, love the chance to express themselves creatively. Art, music, dramatic play, and blocks provide opportunities for children to play where there are no right answers. These activities can often provide a rewarding way to reinforce new skills in many areas. For example, by painting with different colors, a child practices the control of her hands and eyes. If she is learning to count or say color names, you might want to help her count or say the color names as she makes dabs with her paintbrush.

Children with cognitive disabilities benefit from learning routines for play. Teach children routines for different types of play and then always do them. For example, teach children a routine for getting ready to paint: First you roll up your sleeves. Then you put on a smock. Next, you put a paintbrush into each pot of paint. Routines such as these help a child know what to expect and how to play.

On the playground, you might teach a child with cognitive disabilities a routine for getting involved in different kinds of play. For example, you might teach a child to get two plastic shovels on her way out to the playground and then to go to the sandbox and offer another child one of the shovels. They may not play together, but they might sit side by side and dig. As part of the routine, you might teach the child to move to the swings when she tires of the sandbox and from the swings to a climbing structure. You can teach children routines for dramatic play and music, as well as for other types of play.

Adapting Activities for Learning from the World Around Them

*Y*ou won't need to adapt many of the activities for learning about the world for children with cognitive disabilities, but you may need to pay close attention to the safety concerns listed in the Active Learning Series. A child who is likely to touch things and put them into her mouth will need special attention while on a nature walk. Some children may be easily frightened of harmless insects or animals. Such fears are real to the children and deserve your respect.

Watch to see that children use materials appropriately. Because older children are stronger, they may damage toys designed for younger children.

Children with cognitive disabilities may learn a skill in one setting but not be able to use it in other situations or settings. For example, just because a child can tell you that one object is red does not mean that he will be able to tell you that other objects are red. He needs many examples of red objects and many chances to practice finding them on his own.

Active Learning for Children with Physical Disabilities

Jamal has cerebral palsy, so he has a hard time controlling his muscles. He loves the little cars and trucks and the roads, parking garages, and everything else that goes with them, but because he is in a wheelchair most of the time, he can't get on the floor by himself and play with the other children.

The first thing I did was talk to his father about a way to get Jamal out of his wheelchair and onto the floor. After talking to Jamal's physical therapist, we decided that a large wedge-shaped piece of foam was just what we needed. Jamal could lie on his stomach on the foam with his arms and shoulders at the thickest part, kind of hanging over the edge. That left his arms free to play with the toy cars and trucks. It took a while to get the foam, so in the meantime, I rolled up a blanket and put it under Jamal's chest as he lay on his stomach on the floor. Although he got tired in this position after a while, he really enjoyed being on the floor where he could play with the other children, and you wouldn't believe how proud they all were to have him there!

The piece of foam didn't solve all of Jamal's problems, though. Because of his trouble with muscle control, he often knocked over the parking garage, fire station, or whatever was within arm's reach. This sometimes upset the other children, and it certainly didn't make Jamal happy either. To solve this problem, I took a big sheet of stainless steel that I bought at the hardware store. I taped around the sharp edges with heavy-duty tape. On it I super-glued the fire station and parking garage and painted little streets. Then I glued plastic magnetic strips on the bottom of some of the little cars, people, trees, and so forth. This way, Jamal had more success in putting the pieces where he wanted them, and it made it easier for some of the other children, too.

I found out that making things magnetic really helped Jamal play. I bought a huge roll of that magnetic tape and glued it to just about everything. Then I got a stainless steel cookie sheet and attached it with "C" hooks to Jamal's wheelchair, creating his own table. All the toys I had magnetized stuck to the tray, so from that point on, we didn't spend as much time picking up dropped toys for Jamal!

*A*ctive learning is a special challenge for children whose physical disabilities limit their activities. As a caregiver, you will need to be especially creative in adapting activities so that children with physical disabilities can do them.

Infants and children with physical disabilities may not be able to change their positions or move to other areas on their own, so one of your major goals will be to see that the child is placed in different positions and in different areas indoors and out. In addition, many children with physical disabilities require special positioning to allow the normal growth of muscles. The child's parents or physical therapist can advise you about this.

Sometimes people underestimate the abilities of children who have physical disabilities. A child who has difficulty moving her muscles may not be able to show her real skills. This is a frustrating experience and may cause some behavior problems. If a child behaves inappropriately, try to figure out the cause and show understanding and respect for the frustration that causes it.

Because each child's abilities may be very different from every other child with physical disabilities, these tips may have a different meaning for each child.

- *When planning, consider the best space for each activity.* Some spaces will be better than others for positioning children with physical disabilities so that they can take part in activities. The type of floor covering, amount of space in the area, and whether things must be moved may influence your choice. Think about the type of equipment the child may need to participate and whether the space is big enough. Also think about how the child can move into and out of the space as interests and activities change.

- *Position the child so that she is supported, balanced, and safe.* Some young children with physical disabilities will not be able to sit, stand, or walk by themselves. You will want to make it possible for the child to play by supporting the child in some way. You can use a beanbag chair in many ways to support a child. The beanbag is great because all children enjoy using them, so if you have several, the child with disabilities will be right there with all his friends who are using beanbag chairs, too. Avoid using beanbag chairs with infants, however, or with any child whose breathing might be endangered when using this type of chair.

Besides seating the child in the chair, you can also place the child on her side on a mat on the floor with her back resting against the chair for support. In this position, her hands are free to play. Other supports include foam blocks or mats, infant seats, and wheelchairs.

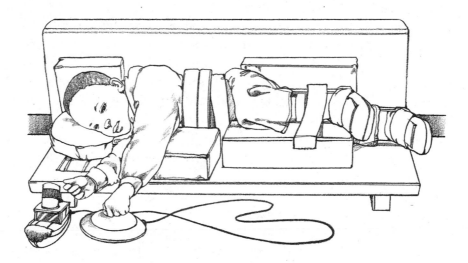

- *Children with physical disabilities should be included in the group and on the same level as the other children.* If the children are on the floor, position the child with physical disabilities on the floor if possible. If children are seated or standing, help the child with physical disabilities assume the same position as part of the group. Avoid placing the child off by himself. For example, when the children are sitting at a table to eat, figure out a way to include the child with physical disabilities at that same table.

- *Change a child's position frequently during the day.* Children get tired of staying in the same position for any length of time. Make sure you put a child in a new position every so often so that she will be comfortable.

Children with physical disabilities may not be able to play with toys unless the toys have been adapted for the children's use. In some cases, the unexpected movements of a child with physical disabilities may knock a toy out of reach.

- *Attach toys to a steady surface.* Some children with physical disabilities may accidentally knock toys out of their reach. There are several solutions to this problem. First, you might hang toys from a bar within the reach of the child. If the child is playing at a table, you might use tape, Velcro, and suction cups to hold toys in place. Larger toys such as a dollhouse can be screwed or glued to a square of plywood. The plywood can then be attached to a table with a C clamp, like those used by carpenters to hold pieces of wood in place.

- *Make key parts of toys, such as handles and buttons, bigger.* Children with physical disabilities will be better able to hold paintbrushes, puzzle pieces, forks and spoons, and other things if they have large handles on them. Use foam handlebar grips from bicycles, sponge hair curlers (minus the rod), or layers of masking tape to make handles bigger. Add handles to puzzle pieces, flat lids, and so forth, by gluing on cork stoppers. Make push buttons larger by gluing a larger piece of plexiglass on top. Make small toys, such as little cars and trucks, easier to pick up by adding handles.

- *Attach switches to battery-operated or plug-in toys.* If a child with physical disabilities can turn a toy on and off, he can participate in many activities that might otherwise not have been possible. For example, a child with severe physical disabilities who has a hard time talking can lead the singing if she can turn a tape recorder on and off. Children who must spend much of their time in wheelchairs can play with battery-powered toys if they are able to operate the switches.

  However, many children with physical disabilities cannot turn the small switches on and off. Some children can only move their heads or arms in large motions, not the small motions needed to turn switches on and off. For such children, toys can be fitted with *adaptive switches.*

  Adaptive switches connect the switch on a toy to a device that the child can use to operate the toy. For example, a joystick can be attached to a tray on a child's wheelchair and then to the switch on a battery-operated truck. Using the joystick, the child can make the truck go in any direction. Figuring out how to increase children's ability to participate in play takes some creativity. For example, by attaching a switch to a small fan, a child can hold a bubble wand in front of the fan and then blow a bubble by turning on the fan. Make sure the holes in the fan cover are too small for children to insert their fingers.

Many different kinds of switches can be attached to toys depending on the child's muscle control. Children can operate switches by whatever motions they can make, such as tilting their heads, blowing, or squeezing. The child's parents or another specialist can often help find someone to design and attach adaptive switches to toys. The Resource List at the end of this section contains information on buying and installing switches.

Typically developing children enjoy using these switches, too; take advantage of this to help the child with the disability be a regular part of the group. Allow all children to use the adapted toys. Then everyone will have lots of things in common.

Adaptive Equipment

Children with physical disabilities often need special equipment to help them get around or to provide support for sitting, standing, or lying. The child's parent, doctor, and physical therapist will decide what kind of equipment a child needs and when it should be used. As children grow and change, the kind of equipment they need will also change.

Active Learning for Children with Disabilities

- *Supports for sitting, standing, and lying.* Some children with physical disabilities need special equipment to support them while they play. A sidelyer is a cushioned mat with pads and straps to comfortably support the child as she lies on her side. This position frees her hands for playing. As a child becomes older, she may use a special chair for sitting. Each chair can look different depending upon the child's needs. Some chairs have supports for a child's head, trunk, and legs. Some chairs have trays attached. Each is designed with an individual child in mind and must be altered as the child grows. Other kinds of supports help a child stand.

- *Equipment to help a child get from one place to another.* Many children with physical disabilities use wheelchairs, walkers, or crutches to help them get around. There are many different kinds of wheelchairs and devices for walking designed to meet the different needs of the children who use them. Braces and splints also help some children walk. These devices can be metal or plastic. The size and type of brace used by a child will change as the child grows bigger and gains new skills.

- *Communication aids.* Communication can be a tremendous challenge for children whose muscles prevent them from forming words. Fortunately, educators and engineers have developed equipment that can help children communicate. One piece of equipment, often called a *communication board,* allows the child to point to symbols for words. Children can point in a number of ways, using a finger, puff of air, or even an eye blink, so that even children with severe physical disabilities can communicate. The symbols on the communication board change as the child grows older and more capable of using complex symbols. Toddlers and preschoolers will have simple picture symbols on their boards that represent the child's ideas or wishes. Children who use communication boards should have access to them at all times.

Adapting Activities for Listening and Talking

*S*ome children with physical disabilities may not have the motor control to speak clearly, although they may understand language just as well as other children. Other children with physical disabilities may have no problem learning to talk. Even though a child may have difficulty learning to talk, she learns to understand what others say when people talk to her. You will not need to do many of the activities in the Active Learning Series differently to help children with physical disabilities learn to use and understand language.

Over time, you will become more able to understand what a child who has trouble talking is saying. Parents can help you understand what their child is saying. Ask a parent to tell you the names of their child's family members, pets, and friends. This way you might be able to guess what a child is saying. Ask parents to tell you about special occasions that the child might want to tell you about, such as birthdays or vacations. When you don't understand a child, ask him to show you or to tell you again.

Some children who have very limited control of their mouths and tongues may use a communication board or computer to communicate. Help other children and adults learn how to understand the messages and respond to them.

Some of the activities for physical development in the Active Learning Series may not be appropriate for children with physical disabilities. Ask the child's parents, doctor, or other professional to go through the Active Learning Series activities with you to talk about which activities would be good for the child.

A child's parents, physical therapist, or doctor may recommend that you encourage the child to move and reach. Many of the activities in the series provide encouragement for children who are reluctant to move.

Ball play. Older children will want to play with balls, just as their friends do. If the child has enough muscle control to catch, you might use a beanbag rather than a ball, since it is easier to catch. A child can catch a ball rolled into outstretched and open legs. If they cannot throw the ball, children in wheelchairs can roll it down a wide chute fastened at one end to their wheelchair.

Climbing. Children love to climb. When they climb, they learn about up and down, over and under, and get a sense of their bodies. Children who cannot get around on their own need help gaining climbing experiences. When possible, lift a child up high, perhaps carrying her on your shoulder. Help a child go through a tunnel or under a climber, perhaps by pulling him in a wagon.

Riding toys. Children with physical disabilities may not be able to balance or pedal a riding toy. If the child can sit on the toy, you might be able to take the child for a ride if you can completely straddle the toy and prevent the child from falling.

Sand and water play. It is easier for a child to play in sand or water if he is standing, so if possible, put the child in a standing position. Have a variety of containers, some of which have handles of different sizes, for children to grip. Attach these toys to the water table with strings, so that if they are dropped, they can be retrieved more easily. Water should be warm, not cold, to increase muscular control.

Adapting Creative Activities

*C*reative activities allow all children to express themselves in satisfying ways. You won't need to change most of the activities for creative expression for children with physical disabilities, but you might need to change the materials in some way or think of new ways for the children to participate. Many of the art activities do not need a great deal of coordination and can be done by children with limited motor control if crayons, washable markers, paintbrushes, and other materials are adapted. Children who are unable to sing can join in by beating a drum or shaking bells. Substituting magnetic blocks for wooden ones can make block activities fun for children with physical disabilities. Children with physical disabilities can participate in dramatic play by wearing hats or clothes to represent a certain role.

*I*ncluding children with physical disabilities may sometimes mean
giving the child a partner. For example, other children in the group
could help a child with physical disabilities collect items from
outside and put them in a bag. Making sure that children with
physical disabilities are in the middle of the action helps them learn
even if they can't actually do the activity themselves.

Active Learning
for Children with
Visual Disabilities

Even with glasses, Luis's vision is very blurred. He can see people and large objects, but has trouble seeing smaller things, such as pictures, leaves, and Duplo™ blocks. Details are also hard for Luis to see unless he is very close. He can't see the expression on people's faces, the designs on the mobile over his crib, or the alphabet wallpaper border in his room.

At 12 months, Luis is sitting and will stand if he's holding on to something, but he doesn't walk yet. He prefers to stay in one place but does crawl sometimes. He isn't ready to do many of the activities for large muscle development in Active Learning for Ones *unless we adapt them in some way because he can't walk or stand alone. For example, the activity "Bend and Look" suggests that adults and children stand in front of a mirror and copy each other's movements. To do this activity, I sit Luis close to the mirror, then I sit behind him and do actions he can do sitting down. If he doesn't copy me, I help him by moving his arms and legs. I changed the activity "Punch the Ball" for Luis, too. In this activity, you put a beach ball in a pillowcase and hang it at the child's eye level, then show him how to punch it. I did this activity with Luis lying down so that he could use both his arms and his legs to hit the ball. I used a bright red pillowcase so that Luis could see it, and inside I put lots of jingle bells in a plastic lidded container so that they would make a noise when Luis hit them.*

Whenever we start a new activity, I spend a few minutes with Luis helping him explore the materials. I guide his hands over items and tell him all about them. When he gets tired of this, I stop.

When we read together, I put Luis in my lap and hold the book close so that he can see the pictures. Next year, I will get some picture books that have braille in them so that Luis can get the idea that braille and reading go together, even though it will be a long time before Luis can read braille.

*C*hildren with visual disabilities are often not attracted to discover the people, events, or things around them because they cannot see. Sometimes, children with visual disabilities seem content to just sit or lie and do nothing. As a caregiver, you will want to be aware of what the child is doing and figure out how you can get him involved in activities.

■ *Give babies and children who are blind lots of touching.* It may seem surprising, but to some children with visual and other disabilities, a firm, gentle touch is preferred to a lighter one. Find out how a child likes to be touched by asking her parents. Although some children do not like to be touched, it is an important way of communicating with young children with visual disabilities. Before touching a child, let her know that you are near and are about to touch her by talking to her in a gentle tone. Even babies need a warning before they are picked up. Massage a baby's arms, legs, and back gently talking to him all the time. Carry a baby with visual disabilities with you wherever you can.

■ *Place babies with visual disabilities on their stomachs to develop the muscles needed for good posture and for reading braille when they are older.*

■ *When a baby is ready, you will need to provide some enticement for the baby to learn to roll over, crawl, and finally walk.* One of your main tasks as a caregiver is to give the child a reason to move—perhaps a musical toy or the sound of your voice. Babies who can see want to move to get to people or objects in their environment. Babies who cannot see or who see poorly may not have any reason to move from one place to another. In fact, moving into space that cannot be seen is frightening, so you can see why some children are content just to stay in one place.

■ *Be kind and patient.* Like most children, a child with a visual impairment will grow to love people who take care of him. The relationship you have with the baby will grow through the feelings you communicate by touch and through your voice.

■ *Help the child with visual disabilities become as independent as possible.* It is easy to understand how children who cannot see could become very dependent on others. Independence is a goal for all children, and as a caregiver, you will want to give a child the assistance she needs to learn a skill, but gradually withdraw the assistance so that the child can become independent. Provide cues that will help the child get around the indoor and outdoor spaces in your child-care setting. The section in this book on environments gives many tips for setting up the environment to help a child with visual disabilities get around independently.

■ *Invite the older preschooler with visual disabilities and her parents into the child-care setting when no one else is there.* Guide her from the door to the different parts of the room. Let her explore the furniture and toys in each area as you talk about them with her. Do the same thing outdoors. Invite the child back as many times as necessary, each time using the same route to get to the different areas in the room. In many cities, specialists are available free of charge to work with caregivers and parents and to help children with visual disabilities learn to move around and become familiar with the various spaces.

■ *To help the child with a visual disability choose what he wants to play with, you might glue an example of the toy on the shelf or box where it is stored so that the child can feel to choose.* For example, you might glue a bead on the box that contains beads for stringing. You might also use textures to distinguish spaces as mentioned in the section on environments in this book.

■ *A child with limited vision may need the right kind of lighting in the room to see.* Some children are very light-sensitive and need protection from bright light; others need bright light in order to see. Ask the child's parents what kind of lighting is best.

■ *When you do activities with children with visual disabilities, guide the child through the motions of the activity.* Stand behind a child and put your hands over her hands to help her hold a crayon, feed herself, or roll a ball. Place a mirror in front of you so that you can see the child's reflection, so that you will know what the child is doing. Describe the activity, using simple words to accompany the movements.

Materials, Equipment, and Toys

*C*hildren with visual disabilities need plenty of toys that they can explore using their other senses, such as hearing and touch. Toys that make noises are especially important for children who have no vision, as well as for children who have limited vision. Children with partial vision will enjoy toys that are brightly colored, light up, or have interesting textures. Buy blocks and balls that have bells inside them, so that they jingle when moved. Many toys that make noises when played with are now commercially available. Shape sorters that whistle when the right shape is placed in a hole and toys that pop out from behind doors when buttons are pressed are also available.

Adaptive equipment designed for children with limited muscle control is also useful for children with visual disabilities. Molded spoons and bowls with a wide lip help children learn to feed themselves. Attaching some toys to a steady surface so that they cannot be accidentally knocked out of reach improves the chances for play.

- Add textures to buttons on equipment. On the tape recorder, paste a square of a different texture on each button. If you have other equipment with on and off buttons, be consistent, always using the same textures for "on" and "off."

- Add sounds to toys by securely attaching bells that are too large to be swallowed.

Adaptive Equipment

Some children with partial vision may wear glasses. It is important to make sure the child wears his glasses whenever he is awake. Very young children who wear glasses will need to have a headstrap to keep them on. Make sure a child's glasses are kept clean and that they continue to fit properly as the child grows.

Conversation. Sighted children experience and understand the expressions on people's faces long before they can talk, but children with visual disabilities do not see this. The expression in your voice can act like the expression on your face. It can communicate a great deal to the child, even if he does not understand your words. When you talk to a child with a visual impairment, put a lot of expression in your voice to communicate your message.

Extra noise near the child can take her attention away from you and what you are saying. When you prepare to do activities for listening and talking with a child with visual disabilities, make sure you are in a quiet area where the child will not be distracted by the activities of children or adults around her.

Help a child with visual disabilities understand that her language will help her control the world around her. Respond quickly to a baby's cries. When the baby begins to coo, coo along with her. As words begin to develop, help children learn words that will get them what they want, such as "juice" and "hug" or the name of a special toy. When the child uses these words, respond quickly by getting the child juice or giving her a hug.

When you introduce the child to something new, talk to her about it in many ways. Go over every part of the object carefully, guiding her hands as you talk. For example, in showing the child around the room, you might first stop at the child's cubby and say, guiding her hands as you speak: *Here is the top of your cubby, and here are the sides, and the bottom. Feel this fuzzy strip on the side? It means that this is your cubby. Now, let's find a hook for your coat. Here it is at the back of the cubby. It is cold and smooth. Feel the ends of the hook? That's the hook that holds up your coat.*

Books and pictures. Pictures help hold the attention of children when you read to them. Children with partial vision can enjoy pictures, too, if they are simple and brightly colored. When showing pictures, allow children with visual disabilities to feel a real object at the same time. If the pictures in the book are line drawings, make bold pictures to go along with them. You might also make large posters to go along with books that all children can enjoy. Draw simple pictures in bright, contrasting colors (light against dark or vice versa). Other books that are specially designed for children with visual disabilities have plastic overlays with braille imprints. Even if they can't read braille, older children can get the idea that braille and reading go together. This helps them get ready to read braille when they are older.

Adapting Activities for Physical Development

By moving around, children learn about their bodies and about the space around them. However, moving into unknown spaces without being able to see what is in that space would be frightening to all of us. It would be especially frightening to lose contact with the ground underneath our feet if we did not know what was around us and how we might get back on solid ground.

As frightening as moving might be for children with visual disabilities, without it, a child will not progress in all developmental areas. Because children with visual disabilities cannot see the world around them, moving through it is one important way of learning about it. They cannot see the arrangement of spaces, so they need to move in it to understand concepts like up and down, in and out, under and over.

Encouraging children with visual disabilities to move around can be hard for caregivers. Caregivers may be afraid that children will hurt themselves. But you can plan carefully to guard against accidents. You can childproof children's spaces—indoors and out—being sure to get rid of all possible dangers.

If the space is safe, you will help the child when you encourage him to take a small risk, rather than protecting him from all mishaps. One way to promote independence safely is to give children fewer supports as they become better at doing things. For example, you might hold the hand of a child while he is learning his way around the room. When he has become familiar with where things are, you might let him hold just your finger to get around the room. As his skills improve, you might hold one end of a piece of string or a scarf while he holds the other. Once the child knows the environment very well, he should be encouraged to explore it independently.

To use the activities in the Active Learning Series you will always need to help a child explore the equipment and materials you are using, and then move her through the motions. For example, to do the "Grabbing Out of a Can" activity, you will need to help the child explore the cubes and the large plastic container first. Then you will need to move the child through the motions of the activity, your hands over hers, for her to understand what to do. Talk gently while you do the activity. The tone of your voice will help the child feel safe and secure.

When an activity uses a visually attractive toy to entice a child to move, substitute a toy that makes a noise. Music and musical instruments can motivate a child to move. For example, to do the "Swinging Colors" activity for babies, choose a toy that makes a noise, such as a bell. Put the bell in the child's hands and show him that moving it makes a noise. Then ring the bell at different places close to the baby. See if he will turn his head or reach out toward the noise. Apply the same ideas to activities for older children.

Playground. Stay close to children with visual disabilities on the playground. Protect them from accidentally walking in front of moving swings or riding toys. It is helpful to mark off a smaller area on the playground where children with visual disabilities can easily and safely get around. Mark this area with brightly colored flags tied to trees or equipment for children who have some sight. Make sure the area contains equipment for children to play with and on but that it is free from things that may cause a child to trip. Encourage one or two other children to play in this space.

Art. If a child has no vision, making art activities interesting means adding textures, smells, even sounds. Use washable markers that have different smells for each color. Add odors to paints (a different one for each color) using bottled flavorings such as lemon and peppermint. (Be sure that the child does not try to eat the paint.) Or paste a different sandpaper shape on each bottle to indicate its color. Adding sand to fingerpaint gives it a gritty feeling that children may prefer over its normal slimy feel. Attaching a screen to a tabletop or easel and then attaching paper over it for coloring gives crayon art an interesting texture.

You will need to move the child through the motions of most art activities. Holding your hand over his, show the older child how to cut, paste, draw, or stick on stickers.

Children with visual disabilities feel more comfortable if they know the boundaries of the space in which they are working, so provide a child with a tray to hold art activities.

Children with little vision have a hard time seeing the faint marks that crayons and pencils make, so let them use washable markers or brightly colored paint instead. Children with visual disabilities will be more likely to see colored glue on white paper. Colored glue is available anywhere you buy crayons and other art supplies, or it can be made by mixing powdered paint or tempera with white glue.

Music. Music is an excellent way to help children with visual disabilities become involved in activities. Action records encourage children to move. Use music as a way to learn all kinds of skills. Make up simple songs to go along with routines such as hanging up coats, taking off shoes, or washing hands. Use the songs to teach routines and also to make routines more fun for children.

Children with visual disabilities want to move when they play musical instruments. Clanging cymbals together helps children learn to get their arms to the middle of their bodies, a skill that sometimes needs training. Tone bells, which make fuller sounds than a toy xylophone, also encourage children to move.

Dramatic play. Planning ahead for dramatic play will help children with visual disabilities be more successful. Talk with other children about including a child with visual disabilities in dramatic play. Think about the role the child will play and how dress-up clothes and other props might be used. Tell the children that they must use words to say what they are doing so that the child with visual disabilities can play, too. Ask one child to make sure that the child with visual disabilities has the props—perhaps eating utensils or dress-up clothes—that he needs to be part of the play.

Adapting Activities for Learning from the World Around Them

*H*earing, touching, tasting, and smelling are the ways in which children with visual disabilities will learn about the world around them. Babies with no sight are completely dependent upon adults to plan activities to help them explore the environment. They will depend mostly on exploring things through touch as an adult talks to them. Babies with some sight can explore the environment if the caregiver is careful to arrange the materials so that the child can see them. The caregiver may need to change the color, size, or location of things so that the child can see them.

Children will learn about spaces best if they can move their whole bodies. When helping children learn "in and out," you might want to find a large box that the child can get in and out of to teach the concepts. Other activities that use the child's whole body—crawling through tunnels, going up steps, stepping over a toy—help children with visual disabilities learn ideas that other children learn by watching.

Older children will enjoy playing simple board games. Adapt games by adding cues that children can feel. Board games that have children move a piece from square to square according to the roll of the dice are difficult for children who have limited sight. Make a spinner with sandpaper dots to use in place of the dice. Use press tape (available at hobby stores) to outline the paths and squares so that children can feel the borders. You might also cut squares out of different textures and place them on the playing board so that a child will know by touch when she's moved from one space to the next.

Active Learning
for Children with
Hearing Loss

Ned always slept well, no matter how much noise his older brother made. To wake him up, his mother had only to touch him or pick him up. Ned smiled and cooed at about the age his brother had, and although Ned's parents were a little worried that he didn't seem to notice some sounds, they were relieved when he began to babble. Because Ned was so quick at learning other skills, his parents really began to worry when, by his first birthday, he didn't seem to understand any words. That's when they discovered he had hearing loss.

Ned wears hearing aids in the child care setting and at home. These help him a great deal, although lots of noise really bothers him when the hearing aids are turned on. He has learned how to take his hearing aids out and does so occasionally, so we really have to watch him. Just like other three-year-old children, Ned can walk, run, and play. We don't have to make many changes in the activities we do in the child-care setting for Ned, but we do make sure that he can see the faces of people who are talking to him. Every day we choose a new buddy for Ned. Sometimes this person is another child, but he or she could also be a caregiver or a volunteer. Ned's buddy makes sure he knows when the cleanup bell rings and helps him when he may not have heard other directions.

*I*t is important to keep listening and talking to children with hearing loss. Doing so will help them learn to communicate. Even though they may never hear what you say, they learn through watching your gestures and your face.

■ *Ask a child's parents how close you must be for the child to be able to hear what you are saying and stay within that distance.* Make sure the child is close to you when you do activities.

■ *Just as you do with hearing children, get down on the level of a child with hearing loss so that she can see your face, and look directly into the face of a baby.*

■ *Notice where a baby's attention is focused and respond to the baby's interest immediately after the baby stops looking at it.* For example, if you notice that a baby is looking at a light, you should allow the baby to look at it without interruption. At the moment the baby shifts attention away from the light, you might say and/or sign, "Light! See, that's a light. It blinks off and on." An adult can get babies to pay attention to something by turning their own body to point to it.

- *Use the same words and simple sentences that you would use with other children of the same age.* If the child doesn't understand, repeat yourself, then simplify the words and sentences. If the child still doesn't understand, point out or demonstrate what you are saying.

- *Talk normally to a child with hearing loss; don't exaggerate your mouth movements.* You may need to speak loudly to children who wear hearing aids. Tell the other children in the room to speak loudly, too, and to touch the child gently when they want his or her attention. If you can, use sign language along with your speech. Facing the child is important since he may not hear if you are beside or behind him.

- *If you have a child who signs, you will want to learn some important signs so that you can communicate with the child.* Sign language is a system of hand signals used to communicate. Sign language is usually used with speaking so that children can learn to lipread and, therefore, understand people who do not use sign language.

- *Be sure the lighting is good in the spaces used by children.* Because children with hearing loss may be learning to lip-read or to use sign language, good lighting is important. When you are talking to a child with hearing loss, try not to stand or sit with the light coming from behind you. If you do, you might look more like a silhouette, and the child won't be able to see your face.

- *Become familiar with the child's hearing aid.* Learn how it operates and how it helps the child hear. Check the battery every day to make sure it is working properly. If a child who wears a hearing aid seems to be missing sounds he usually can hear, check his hearing aid. You may need to do this several times a day.

- *Try to cut down on noise in the room; hearing aids make all sounds in the environment louder, not just the ones that are important.* Use carpets on the floors. Putting thick materials on the wall, such as heavy curtains or foam pads, will also cut down on noise.

- *Remember that you will need to get the attention of a child with hearing loss before you talk to him or give directions.* A gentle tap can signal that it is time to pay attention.

*Y*ou probably won't need to buy or adapt toys for children with hearing loss. Give a child with hearing loss the chance to explore toys that make sounds. The child can feel the vibrations that the toy makes even if he or she cannot hear the sound.

Adaptive Equipment

- *Hearing aids.* A hearing aid helps a child hear by making sounds louder—all sounds, including toys being dumped onto the floor, people walking, traffic, and so forth. Sometimes all this noise keeps the child from hearing what is really important.

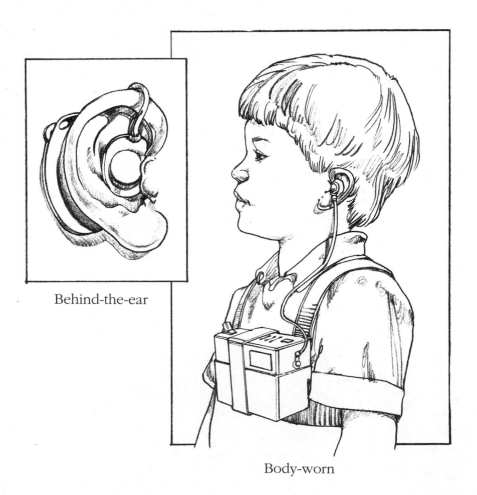

Behind-the-ear

Body-worn

There are two kinds of hearing aids worn by children. One type is worn behind the ear. The other type looks like a small box and is worn on the body in a harness.

How well hearing aids help children to hear depends on the type and severity of the child's hearing loss. Some children are able to understand spoken words with the help of a hearing aid. Others may hear only some of what is said. For other children, hearing aids may only let them know that a sound is being made.

You should check the hearing aid every day. Ask the child's parent to show you how. Keep the hearing aid dry and clean. Make sure hearing aids that are worn in a harness are covered by a waterproof smock when the child is playing in the water or painting.

Children should wear their hearing aids all the time. Some parents are afraid that their child might lose the hearing aid. Let them know the importance of allowing the child to wear it all the time and that they can get insurance that will cover the cost of replacement if it is lost.

Most activities in the Active Learning Series can be carried out without many adaptations for children with hearing loss. You will simply need to talk with children as outlined in the *Here's How* section on page 129. However, here are some ideas that you might find helpful when you plan activities for listening and talking, as well as music and dramatic play activities, so that children with hearing loss can be fully included.

Books and pictures. Babies with hearing loss will enjoy looking at pictures and books. Remember to let the child look as long as he wants. When he changes his focus, get his attention and say or sign the words. When you are reading to an older child with hearing loss, make sure you stop reading to give the child time to look away from your face to see the pictures without missing any of the story.

Conversation. Talk to babies as you hold them. Even though a baby with hearing loss may not hear the words, she may feel the vibrations of your speech when you are holding her. A particularly good activity for a baby with hearing loss is "Watching Talking" (*Active Learning for Infants,* number 28). Placing the baby on your lap facing you allows the baby to experience sound through feeling it.

The activities in the Active Learning Series for conversation with older children can be carried out with children with hearing loss if you follow the advice given in the *Here's How* section. Make sure you give the child a chance to speak in group activities. Look for signals that the child has something to say and then help the other children give him a turn. Give the child time to start and finish speaking, and do not correct his pronunciation. You may sometimes need to help the other children understand what the child with hearing loss is saying by interpreting or repeating what he says.

Music. Children with hearing loss can participate in music activities. Even though they may not be able to hear musical notes, they can feel the beat of the music. Show children with hearing loss how to beat a drum or move in time with the music. Hold an infant in your arms while music is being played and move around in time with the beat. You may even want to dance as you hold the baby securely in your arms.

Children with hearing loss who talk may be able to participate in singing if you teach them the words to the song, even if they don't hit all the notes. Other children with hearing loss can tap a drum in time with the music or sign the words. Other children in the program will enjoy learning signs for words in their songs.

Dramatic Play. For older children, dramatic play is often a time when children play together. In these situations and in others where the child is playing with other children, there are some things you can do to make sure a child with hearing loss is included. First of all, make sure the child knows when she is being asked to join in the play. You can tell the child yourself that other children are asking her to play, or you can tell one of the hearing children to get close to her and tell her. Make sure children with hearing loss understand the rules of play. What role does the child have? What is she supposed to do? Stay nearby until you are sure she understands. You may also need to interpret for the child during play if her speech is hard for others to understand.

When You Want
to Know More

BOOKS AND ARTICLES

Bailey, D. B., and M. Wolery. *Teaching Infants and Preschoolers with Disabilities,* 2d ed. New York: Macmillan, 1992.

Batshaw, M. L., and Y. M. Perrett, *Children with Disabilities: A Medical Primer,* 3d ed. Baltimore: Paul H. Brooks, 1992.

Brault, L. M. J. "Achieving integration for infants and toddlers with special needs: Recommendations for practice." *Infants and Young Children,* 5 (2) (1992), pp. 78–85.

Cryer, D., T. Harms, and B. Bourland. *Active Learning for Infants.* Menlo Park, CA: Addison-Wesley, 1987.

———. *Active Learning for Ones.* Menlo Park, CA: Addison-Wesley, 1987.

———. *Active Learning for Twos.* Menlo Park, CA: Addison-Wesley, 1988.

———. *Active Learning for Threes.* Menlo Park, CA: Addison-Wesley, 1988.

"Encouraging social interaction through play." *Child Care Plus,* 2(1), (Fall 1991).

Hanline, M. F., and M. Bair. *Supported Transition to Integrated Preschools.* San Francisco: San Francisco Unified School District, 1988.

Harms, T., and R. M. Clifford. *Early Childhood Environment Rating Scale.* New York: Teachers College Press, 1980.

———. *Family Day Care Rating Scale.* New York: Teachers College Press, 1989.

Harms, T., D. Cryer, and R. M. Clifford. *Infant/Toddler Environment Rating Scale.* New York: Teachers College Press, 1990.

Hatton, D. "Services for young children with visual handicaps in North Carolina." *In-Tac Tribune,* V(5) (1992), pp. 1–4.

"Healthy child care for children with disabilities." *Child Care Plus,* 1(4) (Summer 1991).

"Integrated child care: What it is and what it isn't." *Child Care Plus,* 1(1) (Fall 1990).

Johnson-Martin, N. M., S. M. Attermeier, and B. Hacker, *The Carolina Curriculum for Preschoolers with Special Needs*. Baltimore: Paul H. Brookes, 1990.

Learner, J., C. Mardell-Czudnowski, and D. Goldenberg. *Special Education for the Early Childhood Years,* 2d ed. Englewood Cliffs, NJ: Prentice Hall, 1987.

Lovell, P., and T. Harms. "How can playgrounds be improved?" *Young Children,* March 1985.

Mainstreaming preschoolers: Children with emotional disturbance. DHEW Publication No. OHDS 78-31115. Project Head Start, Washington, DC: U.S. Government Printing Office.

Mainstreaming preschoolers: Children with health impairments. Project Head Start, DHEW Publication No. OHDS 78-31111. Washington, DC: U.S. Government Printing Office.

Mainstreaming preschoolers: Children with hearing impairments. Project Head Start. DHEW Publication No. OHDS 78-31116. Washington, DC: U.S. Government Printing Office.

Mainstreaming preschoolers: Children with mental retardation. Project Head Start. DHEW Publication No. OHDS 78-31110. Washington, DC: U.S. Government Printing Office.

Mainstreaming preschoolers: Children with orthopedic handicaps. Project Head Start. DHEW Publication No. OHDS 78-31114. Washington, DC: U.S. Government Printing Office.

Mainstreaming preschoolers: Children with speech and language impairments. Project Head Start. DHEW Publication No. OHDS 78-31113. Washington, DC: U.S. Government Printing Office.

Mainstreaming preschoolers: Children with visual handicaps. Project Head Start. DHEW Publication No. OHDS 78-31112. Washington, DC: U.S. Government Printing Office.

Martin, S. S., M. P. Brady, and R. E. Williams. "Effects of toys on the social behavior of preschool children in integrated and nonintegrated groups: Investigation of a setting event." *Journal of Early Intervention,* 15(2) (1991), pp.153–161.

Meisels, S. J. *Special Education and Development*. Baltimore: University Park Press, 1979.

Mulligan, S. A., et al. *Integrated Child Care*. Tucson, AZ: Communication Skill Builders, 1992.

Musselwhite, C. R. *Adaptive Play for Special Needs Children.* San Diego: College Hill Press, 1986.

Neisworth, J. T., and R. R. Fewell, eds. [Special issue] "Mainstreaming revisited." *Topics in Early Childhood Education,* 10(2) (Summer 1990).

Odom, S. L., et al. *The Integrated Preschool Curriculum.* Seattle: University of Washington Press, 1988.

Odom, S. L., S. R. McConnell, and M. A. McEvoy. *Social Competence of Young Children with Disabilities.* Baltimore: Paul H. Brookes, 1992.

Osborne, S., B. Kniest, C. Garland, D. Moore, and D. Usry. *SpecialCare Curriculum and Trainers' Manual.* Lightfoot, VA: Child Development Resources, 1993.

Peck, C. A., P. Carlson, and E. Helmstetter. "Parent and teacher perceptions of outcomes for typically developing children enrolled in integrated early childhood programs: A statewide study." *Journal of Early Intervention,* 16(1) (1992), pp. 53–63.

Peterson, N. L. *Early Intervention for Handicapped and At-Risk Children: An Introduction to Early Childhood–Special Education.* Denver: Love Publishing Co., 1987.

"The accessible child care environment". *Child Care Plus,* 1(2) (Winter 1991).

"The universal playground." *Exceptional Parent,* October 1990.

Weinstein, C. S., and T. G. David. *Spaces for Children.* New York: Plenum Press, 1987.

Wesley, P. W. *Mainstreaming Young Children: A Training Series for Child Care Providers.* Chapel Hill, NC: Frank Porter Graham Child Development Center, 1992.

Wolery, M., P. S. Strain, and D. B. Bailey. "Applying the framework of developmentally appropriate practice to children with special needs." In *Reaching Potentials: Appropriate Curriculum and Assessment for Young Children* by S. Bredekamp and T. Rosegrant, eds., pp. 92–112. Washington, DC: National Association for the Education of Young Children, 1992.

AGENCIES

For Children with Disabilities

Association of Birth Defect Children
3526 Emerywood Lane
Orlando, FL 32806

The Exceptional Parent
1170 Commonwealth Avenue, 3rd floor
Boston, MA 01234
(617) 536-8961

March of Dimes
Public Health Education and Community Services Department
1275 Mamaroneck Avenue
White Plains, NY 10605

National Early Childhood Technical Assistance System (NECTAS)
The University of North Carolina at Chapel Hill
CB# 8040, 500 NCNB Plaza
Chapel Hill, NC 27514
(919) 962-2001

National Information Center for Children and Youth with Disabilities
P.O. Box 1492
Washington, DC 20013
(800) 999-5599

Sibling Information Network
Connecticut's University Affiliated Program on Developmental Disabilities
991 Main Street
East Hartford, CT 06108
(203) 282-7050

For Specific Health Impairments

Alliance of Genetic Support Groups
38th and R Streets, NW
Washington, DC 20057

American Cancer Society
90 Park Avenue
New York, NY 10016

American Juvenile Arthritis Organization
1314 Spring Street, NW
Atlanta, GA 30309

Aplastic Anemia Foundation of America
P.O. Box 22689
Baltimore, MD 21203

Asthma and Allergy Foundation of America
1717 Massachusetts Avenue, NW, Suite 305
Washington, DC 20036

The Candlelighters Childhood Cancer Foundation
2025 I Street, NW
Washington, DC 20006

Cystic Fibrosis Foundation
6931 Arlington Road
Bethesda, MD 20814

Epilepsy Foundation of America
4351 Garden City Drive
Landover, MD 20785

Juvenile Diabetes Foundation International
432 Park Avenue South, 16th floor
New York, NY 10016

Leukemia Society of America
733 Third Avenue
New York, NY 10017

National Digestive Diseases Information Clearinghouse
1255 23rd Street, NW, Suite 275
Washington, DC 20037

National Hemophilia Foundation
Soho Building
110 Greene Street, Room 406
New York, NY 10012

National Kidney Foundation
30 East 33rd Street
New York, NY 10016

National Association for Sickle Cell Disease
4221 Wilshire Boulevard
Los Angeles, CA 90010-3503

National Tay-Sachs and Allied Diseases Association, Inc.
385 Elliott Street
Newton, MA 02164

For Speech and Language Impairments	American Cleft Palate-Craniofacial Association 1218 Grandview Avenue Pittsburgh, PA 15211
	American Cleft Palate Educational Foundation (ACPEF) 331 Salk Hall University of Pittsburgh Pittsburgh, PA 15261
For Behavior Problems	Autism Services Center Douglass Education Building Tenth Avenue and Bruce Street Huntington, WV 25701
	Autism Society of America 1234 Massachusetts Avenue, NW, Suite 1017 Washington, DC 20005
For Visual Impairments	Affiliated Leadership League of and for the Blind of America 2025 I Street, NW, Suite 405 Washington, DC 20006
	American Foundation for the Blind 15 West 16th Street New York, NY 10011
	American Alliance for Health, Physical Education, Recreation and Dance P.O. Box 10375 Alexandria, VA 22310
	Blind Children's Center 4120 Marathon Street Los Angeles, CA 90029-0159
	Blind Children's Fund 230 Central Street Auburndale, MA 02116-2399
	National Association for the Visually Handicapped 22 West 21st Street New York, NY 10010
	National Federation of the Blind 1800 Johnson Street Baltimore, MD 21230

National Society to Prevent Blindness
79 Madison Avenue
New York, NY 10016

Visual Foundation, Inc.
818 Mt. Auburn Street
Watertown, MA 02172

For Physical Disabilities
American Academy for Cerebral Palsy and Developmental Medicine
2405 Westwood Avenue, Suite 205
P.O. Box 11083
Richmond, VA 23230

American Brittle Bone Society
1256 Merrill Drive
Marshallton
West Chester, PA 19380

Muscular Dystrophy Association
810 Seventh Avenue
New York, NY 10019

Osteogenesis Imperfecta Foundation, Inc.
P.O. Box 14807
Clearwater, FL 34629-4807

Spina Bifida Association of America
1700 Rockville Pike, Suite 540
Rockville, MD 20852

United Cerebral Palsy Association
7 Penn Plaza, Suite 804
New York, NY 10001

For Hearing Loss
Alexander Graham Bell Association for the Deaf
3417 Volta Place, NW
Washington, DC 20007

American Society for Deaf Children and the
  National Association for the Deaf
814 Thayer Avenue
Silver Spring, MD 20910

Consumers Organization for the Hearing Impaired, Inc.
c/o National Association for Hearing and Speech Action
10801 Rockville Pike
Rockville, MD 20852

John Tracy Clinic
West Adams Boulevard
Los Angeles, CA 90007

National Information Center on Deafness
Gallaudet University
800 Florida Avenue, NW
Washington, DC 20002

For Cognitive Disabilities

American Association for Mental Retardation
1719 Kalorama Road, NW
Washington, DC 20009

Association for Children with Down Syndrome
2616 Martin Avenue
Bellmore, NY 11710

Association for Retarded Citizens of the United States
National Headquarters
2501 Avenue J
Arlington, TX 76005

National Down Syndrome Congress
1800 Dempster Street
Park Ridge, IL 60068-1146

National Down Syndrome Society
141 Fifth Avenue
New York, NY 10010

National Tuberous Sclerosis Association, Inc.
National Headquarters
P.O. Box 612
Winfield, IL 60190

Prader-Willi Syndrome Association
6490 Excelsior Boulevard, Room 102
St. Louis Park, MN 55426

For Families of
Children with
Disabilities

Family Resource Coalition
230 N. Michigan Avenue, Suite 162
Chicago, IL 60601

The Family Survival Project
1736 Divisadero Street
San Francisco, CA 94115

National Maternal and Child Health Resource Center
College of Law Building
University of Iowa
Melrose and Byington
Iowa City, IA 52242
(319) 335-9067

Parent Care
University of Utah Medical Center
Suite 2A210
Salt Lake City, UT 84132

Parents Helping Parents
47 Maro Drive
San Jose, CA 95127

Parents of Premature and High Risk Infants International, Inc.
33 West 42nd Street
New York, NY 10036

Sibling and Adult Children's Network
2101 Wilson boulevard, Suite 302
Arlington, VA 22201

Materials to Order

About Play Activities for Children with Disabilities

Note: The following information was compiled in part from entries in *Adaptive Play for Special Needs Children: Strategies to Enhance Communication and Learning* (1986) by Caroline Ramsey Musselwhite, College Hill Press, San Diego, CA. This book in its entirety is recommended for anyone caring for children with disabilities.

Art Activities for the Handicapped (1982) by S. M. Atack.
Communication Skill Builders
P.O. Box 42050-J
Tucson, AZ 85733

Learning Through Art. (1975) by J. H. Campbell, M. P. King, and M. Robson.
DLM/Teaching Resources
P.O. Box 4000
Allen, TX 75502

Learning Through Play: A Resource Manual for Teachers and Parents, Birth to Three Years (1983) by R. R. Fewel and P. F. Vadasy.
DLM/Teaching Resources
P.O. Box 4000
Allen, TX 75002

Learning to Talk is Child's Play (1982) by C. Ausberger, M. Martin, and J. Creighton.
Communication Skill Builders
P.O. Box 42050-J
Tucson, AZ 85733

Let Me Play (1977) by D. Jeffree, R. McConkey, and S. Hewson.
Souvenir Press (Educational and Academic) Ltd.
43 Great Russell Street
London, England, WCIB
(published in Canada by Methuen Publications, Agincourt, Ontario)

Prattle and Play: Equipment Recipes for Nonspeech Communication (1982) by F. Carlson.
Media Resource Center
Meyer Children's Rehabilitation Institute
University of Nebraska Medical Center
Omaha, NE 68131

Songbook: Signs and Symbols for Children (1985) by C. R. Musselwhite.
Developmental Equipment
981 Winnetka Terrace
Lake Zurich, IL 60047.

About Adapting Toys for Children

Homemade Battery Powered Toys and Educational Devices for Severely Handicapped Children (1980) by L. J. Burkhart.
Linda J. Burkhart
8303 Rhode Island Avenue
College Park, MD 20740

Making Toys for Handicapped Children: A Guide for Parents and Teachers (1981) by R. McConkey and D. Jeffree.
Prentice Hall
Englewood Cliffs, NJ 07632

More Handmade Battery Devices for Severely Handicapped Children and Suggested Activities. (1980) by L. J. Burkhart (see address above).

Touch Toys and How to Make Them (1981) by H. Z. ten Horn.
Touch Toys, Inc.
P.O. Box 2224
Rockville, MD 20852
Note: This book shows how to use household items to make toys for children with visual impairments.

ToyBrary Catalogue (1978) by R. C. Webb.
Media/Library
Nebraska Diagnostic Resource Centre
1910 Meridian
Cozad, NE 68130

Toys and Play for Handicapped Children (1982) by B. Riddick.
Croom Helm
51 Washington Street
Dover, NH 03820

Toys Help: A Guide to Choosing Toys for Handicapped Children (1981).
Canadian Association of Toy Libraries
1207-50 Quebec Avenue
Toronto, Ontario M6P484
Canada

About the Child-Care Environment

Adventure Playgrounds for Handicapped Children (1978).
Handicapped Adventure Playground Association
Fulham Palace, Bishops Avenue
London, SW6 6EA, England 45

Playgrounds for Free (1974) by P. Hogan.
MIT Press
28 Carleton Street
Cambridge, MA 02142

Principals of Playground Design (film) (1978).
University of South Florida
Film Library
4202 Fowler Avenue
Tampa, FL 33620

About Storybooks that Show Children with Disabilities in a Positive Light

*Health, Illness, and Disability: A Guide to Books for Children and Young
 Adults* (1984) by P. Asarnoff.
Pediatric Projects, Inc.
P.O. Box 1880
Santa Monica, CA 90406